Contents

Preface

With the current explosive growth in television channels, the demand for more and more presenters continues to increase. Although the competition for each job is as great as ever, there are skills which can be learnt that will put you ahead of the game. It may appear, at first glance, that anyone can be a TV presenter. However, after a short spell of channel-hopping, it soon becomes apparent that successful presenters have something special – a magnetic personality, perhaps, or a specialist knowledge (how much do *you* know, for example, about the anatomy of the great white shark, the mysteries of the stock market, dolls hospitals, wild desert orchids or even paper clips? Indeed, there are a whole myriad of interests explored on TV which reflect every aspect of our lives on and off this planet.

TV presenters come from many different backgrounds – they may be actors, journalists, sportspeople, media students, doctors, disc jockeys or plumbers – but they all need personality and commitment. Thousands of people want to be presenters, and the more free and easy the style of the presenter, the more people think, 'Hey, I could do that.' We see filming on the streets, and the everyday use of personal camcorders, so how can it be that difficult? In fact, making something look easy is a skill in itself; and whilst charisma and personality may get you through the studio door, you'll need know-how and professionalism to help you stay there. It's important to acquire skills which will enable you to continue to work well when the pressure is on.

TV presenting skills aren't exclusively required by broadcast networks, as the corporate world now recognises. At major conferences it has become more and more common to include video presentations or live links with managing directors, financiers and specialists giving reports from their offices around the world. There is an increasing need for direct and instant information. Video conferencing and Internet communication has put the corporate world on screen in the office space. Fortunately, many of the same TV presentation skills and guidelines also apply in this field of media use.

This book, then, is intended as a guide for everyone with an interest in television, video or on-screen presentation. It is written from my own personal experience of presenting and coaching new presenters, both for television and for business, and includes practical exercises throughout which – as well as being fun – will help develop your presenting skills. Please do them! I believe that the way to learn is to get up and do it yourself.

The first chapters examine how you can develop your confidence and your own individual style, recognise what works especially well for you, and identify where you feel most comfortable and which aspect you may wish to change. This is followed by a section on preparing the presenter for the studio. Once in front of the cameras the technical aspects of presenting are explored – who does what, the presenter's responsibilities, and lots more. Read and absorb what you need. You may think some codes of practice rigid and some not applicable to your form of presentation. Every rule has an exception, so think of the information set out here as a guideline – a framework to which you can always refer. Once you have a clear understanding of the ground rules you can start to develop your skills and have fun experimenting with new ideas, revealing your individual flair and style. Of course, it would be unfair to leave you without some ideas on how to launch yourself into a TV presenting career, so I have included some suggestions to see you on your way.

Welcome to the world of TV presenting!

Joanne Zorian-Lynn

Part One

BECOMING A TV PRESENTER

1

Introduction

So you want to be a TV presenter. The question has to be asked – why? Here's just a selection of common replies:

- I want to be famous
- I want to be on TV
- I want to be rich
- Anyone can do it
- It looks like fun and it's better than working
- It's the only thing I've ever wanted to do.

First, let's dispel some myths. Fame as a TV presenter can only be achieved by a few. There are many working TV presenters, but fame and fortune is only attained by those who have good contacts, who are single-mindedly determined – and, ultimately, who get a lucky break. There are some people who become famous for reasons completely divorced from TV presenting: for example, top clothes designers, chefs, politicians cited in fraud scandals, jilted lovers of sports personalities, etc., who are then offered a TV show of their own. For them, a door of opportunity opens to a whole new career. However, in common with everyone else, unless they can perform with skill and personality that door will very quickly slam shut. Then, there is the fact that with fame comes press and media intrusion into your personal life. There's no way of getting around this – if you want to be in the public eye, you have to accept that you cannot lay down conditions.

Wanting to be on TV in itself is not enough. If your true desire is to be noticed or to feel important in life, then this is the wrong career for you. TV presenting is about communication, not self-gratification. Ask yourself what you are actually offering to the viewer. What do you want to share with them? Remember that the world of TV presenting can be a cruel one, and you will need to be prepared for heavy and even unreasonable criticism because unfortunately, everyone is a critic. Many feel it is their 'duty' to tell you what they think, no matter how unfair it may seem to you. Debbie Greenwood, TV presenter says, 'You have to develop a thick skin.' Because the competition is so great you will have to accept that as well as the good times there will be many setbacks and rejections. Sometimes you will be unsuccessful because your hair is the wrong colour, or because the producer advertised for a tall, black, male presenter and then decided halfway through the auditions that what was needed was three blonde, female presenters and a cute kid! The trick is not to take it personally.

Big financial rewards come only to a fortunate few, and they still have to work for it. No one pays you for just being there. TV networks are businesses and they'll want something more than just a pretty face. Of course, a pretty or handsome face is a bonus and may well get you a screen test, even the odd show, but if you can't do the job you'll be out. Even if you are lucky enough to land a long contract there is no such thing as job security: at times you'll be inundated with offers and then at others you'll think that you'll never work again. The natural consequence of that is a lack of regular income. However, cable and digital production houses offer plenty of excellent opportunities for new presenters and pay decent, if not extravagant, salaries. Good money can also be made presenting corporate videos. If you fit this niche it's an excellent avenue to explore, although it is still a competitive world and to keep working you'll need a professional edge.

Anyone can do it, can't they? Well, yes, so it would seem. After all, even home video clips, personal views and video diaries make it on to network TV. But you don't have to be a broadsheet critic to differentiate between the amateur and the professional – between the presenter who makes untoward mistakes, speaking without belief in what they're saying, and the presenter who is confident and makes you feel at ease. Which one do you want to be? A presenter needs to find a balance between ease and formality, between honesty and objectivity, whilst at the same time working within a technical and time-limited framework.

If you think that it's all fun and glamour, consider the long, unsociable hours, the inevitably long delays during technical preparations, or the tedious waiting in a studio or damp field for the appearance of your interviewee. Then there are the constant changes in your schedule, both professional and personal. This is not a 'nine to five' job, a fact that you may consider to be a benefit; but alterations to the planned day can happen at a moment's notice and consequently have an effect on every area of your life. You'll need understanding friends, family and partners to cope with cancelled dates, parties and holidays as you put your job first.

Now you know some home truths it is time to herald the great benefits which are certainly attainable for the successful. Here some TV presenters say it for themselves.

'I love the adrenalin rush of the countdown to going live. And the unpredictability of a story breaking on air. You are really at the cutting edge of news.'
Kirsty Lang (Channel 4 News)

'I love it. It's a short-lived career if you just want to be on telly, though – you'll easily get bored if the job isn't what you are interested in.'
Lisa Aziz (SKY News and BBC Big Talk)

'I didn't really want to do anything else. I was always very focused. Each job is different and I love the number of people you meet.'
Kirsten O'Brien (BBC Youth Programmes – formerly CBBC presenter)

'I've always been incredibly, passionately excited by TV. I read books on how programmes were made. I really got the bug about wanting to work in TV, and it's never left me. I'm having the best time of my life.'
Jeff Moody (Channel 5 Weather)

'I love being able to help people plan their lives, giving information which affects them.'
Siân Lloyd (TV weather presenter)

'I still can't believe I get paid for having such a good time. Go for it. You get to travel the world. You're never bored. It's a wonderful life.'
Paul Coia (BBC Pebble Mill, Catchword – formerly senior continuity announcer at Channel 4)

WHAT QUALITIES AND SKILLS DO YOU NEED?

There is no way you can underestimate the competition you will face for each presenting job, but – as this book will demonstrate – there are a number of factors that can put you ahead of the game. Here is a summary of them.

The qualities

- To always be ready for anything – on and off the set
- To be forever optimistic
- To be good natured
- To have patience
- To be flexible and adaptable to change at a moment's notice
- To be able to put on a happy face when you're feeling like death
- To be able to look and sound fresh and cheerful for the 22nd take, even when it's not your fault
- To be able to take harsh professional and personal criticism, identifying that which is justifiable and valuable and that which is not
- To be ready to listen and take direction
- To be creative and able to make suggestions, not demands
- To be co-operative and stay out of everyone's way until you're needed
- To be able to relax, and appear to be relaxed
- To be happy to be yourself
- To laugh at yourself.

The skills

- To be able to sight-read
- To be able to make sense of poorly written scripts
- To be able to make scriptwriters' words sound like your own
- To make a complicated text or concept understandable to the viewer
- To be able to rewrite scripts, adding in new information
- To be able to summarise a piece of text or interview with confidence and clarity to camera
- To be able to 'ad lib' and fill in to time
- To be able to judge time and have a good mental clock
- To be able to learn lines quickly
- To not be distracted by a director's instructions, out-of-vision activity or technical breakdowns
- To acquire a wide general knowledge so that you have an understanding, show genuine interest and can speak with coherence on a variety of subjects
- To acquire and practise good vocal skills
- To be able to cat nap.

2

You, the Presenter

Being natural and at ease in front of the camera is an essential ability, and yet being yourself can be the hardest challenge. People often have a false image of themselves based on a desire to be someone else, when in fact the person that they really are is brimming with attractive qualities. Before you read on, stand in front of a mirror, take a moment to look at yourself, stand up tall and tell yourself that you're gorgeous, glamorous, sexy, superior, empowered and talented. OK, done it? Good. Best to get that over and done with, because although it might be true, no-one's interested in your smug ego. What's more, it gets in the way of your work. It's imperative to have personality and confidence, but temper it with good humour or you may alienate your audience. Unless you can be naturally 'you', the viewer will turn off.

> 'Be yourself and see if you like what you see. Nurture what you've got yourself, rather than trying to be like someone else – someone you *want* to be. In a live situation, if something goes wrong or you forget your lines, the only way to cope is by being yourself. There's nothing to hide.'
> *Kevin Duala (Holiday Programme)*

So where do you start?

REVEALING THE TRUE YOU

Focus on your own personal qualities, skills and abilities. To successfully market yourself you need to be sure of who you are. Under stress, it's very easy to let a mask slip. So don't wear one.

EXERCISES
(1)   Ask yourself these questions:
      What sort of a presenter do you think you are?
      Are you a lively, bouncy sort of presenter? Are you straight
      and informative? Are you a comedian?

5

Then write down a description of the style of presenter that you believe fits you best.

(2) Look at the menu of programme styles listed in the box below. Which you do think would suit you best?

Programme Styles

- Straight, non-committal news style – current affairs
- Investigative journalism
- Documentary
- Informative – travel, gardening, scientific, financial, historical, geographical
- Chatty, on-the-sofa magazine style
- Games show, quiz show
- Facilitated discussion and interview – hard news, lifestyle
- Entertainment – music, comedy, movies
- 'Off the wall' – zany, mad
- Children's programmes
- Educational

---

(3) What sort of programmes do you think would be fun to present. Would you be a suitable presenter? If not, why not?

(4) Every TV programme requires a different style and therefore requires different presenters to suit each style.
Write down the name of a programme which fits appropriately with each of these styles. Name the presenter of each programme. Then shuffle them about so that the news reader becomes a game-show host, the quirky children's presenter takes on the 10 o'clock news, and so on. It's a fun exercise, simply because their own particular brand of presenting doesn't quite fit another style of programme.

In the normal course of TV presenting, it's impossible to be every style of presenter – so do not try to be. More often than not a presenter who is trying to be cool, isn't and trying to be outrageous can just look silly. Find the presenter that's *you*. Find your own style, your own brand. What suits you best? What do you want to be known for? Identify your presentation style, feel at ease and be comfortable with it. Be yourself.

FINDING OUT MORE ABOUT YOU

EXERCISES

(1) List 10 areas – including sports, interests and pastimes – in which you have good knowledge.

1. _____   6. _____

2. _____   7. _____

3. _____   8. _____

4. _____   9. _____

5. _____   10. _____

Select the three at which you are most skilled, or in which you are most interested.

1. _____   3. _____

2. _____

(2) Name 10 of your fantastic qualities! Not your presenting abilities – facts about you and your personality.

1. _____   6. _____

2. _____   7. _____

3. _____   8. _____

4. _____   9. _____

5. _____   10. _____

Choose the three which you feel most comfortable with. There are no judgements to be made here: it's something for you to take on board and feel good about.

1. _____   3. _____

2. _____

As you gain experience and grow, you'll find qualities you didn't know you had and be delighted in them.

DEFINING YOU, THE PRESENTER

EXERCISES

(1) What characteristic(s) will make people want to watch you? Is there anything that marks you out as different from other presenters?

_____

_____

(2) What have you done recently that would make people interested in you? (This could be professional or social.)

_____

_____

(3) Think of yourself as a well-known product on the market. What would be the name of your company or brand?

Write yourself a punchy one-liner. For instance:

- A shoe company – '*Stomp* – the shoe that's going places.'
- A magazine – 'Separate the fact from the fiction. Read *Reality*. Out now.'
- A soft drink – _____
- A computer game – _____

Now – you, the presenter. What are you offering? Write a punchy one-liner, selling *you*.

_____

(4) Imagine that you have your own TV show. Visualise it.

- What sort of programme is it?
- Visualise the titles.
- Hear the opening music.
- Visualise the set.
- What items are on the programme?

Now write your own promo (promotional) – also known as a voice trail or voice commercial – in 20–25 words (7–8 seconds):

That's just one of the many programmes that you could present. I know of one presenter who appears in a magazine chat show, an all-action quiz, a DIY programme and a travel show . . . but her own style remains the same.

So, by now you should be starting to get a clear picture of 'you, the presenter'. Your style should start to become inbuilt so that you can get on with the job from a very grounded position. As the TV world is so competitive, you will need to keep an eye on the way in which industry demands and styles change. It's important to note that there are constant improvements in technology, so you must be ready to respond to these developments. Presenting styles change, sometimes very quickly, and it's your responsibility to be aware of them and know which programmes are incorporating the new trends so that you can subtly build them into your own presentation style.

THE ROLE OF THE PRESENTER

When I started as a TV announcer (some call it 'continuity' or 'anchor' – see also pp. 123-8), I was reminded that I was the 'host' for the station. Very often a presenter is called the host – 'Your host tonight is . . .' – because they are welcoming and inviting the viewer to share the show with them. And, like at any party, the guest (i.e. the viewer) wants to feel 'catered for', involved. Matthew Kelly, presenter of *Stars in Their Eyes* and *Game for a Laugh*, puts it this way: 'Convince your audience that you are trustworthy enough to take them through the evening.'

As a presenter, it's up to you to make sure that everyone is comfortable; the audience wants to feel safe in your hands. It doesn't matter if it's a straight news-read or a wacky 'anything goes' show – you are still the host. You're the bridge between guests, programme content and audience, and it's important that you remember to fulfil that role. It can be very easy to get carried away in the enjoyment of it all and in being centre of the attention, but the viewer hasn't tuned in to watch you turn yourself on – they want to see that you're in control, and that they can relate to you on some level. Remember, too, that there's a whole gallery of folk – directors, vision mixers, sound engineers – who are *really* in control. Always bear in mind that you are a part of a team. There's a lot of people involved in programme-making and just because you are in vision and getting the 'star' attention does not mean that you can disregard the needs of others. That way trouble lies. Keep that ego in check: it may be your downfall.

As well as being the host and link for the audience, you are the bringer of news, information and entertainment. The viewer trusts you. They have no reason to doubt you – unless you give them one. You can do that in several ways:

- By being false to yourself
- By being uneasy with yourself or with your programme material
- By being nervous
- By presenting mixed messages with your image
- By poor vocal delivery.

REMEMBER WHO YOU'RE TALKING TO

Don't generalise. You are not talking to thousands or millions of people. First of all, that's too scary to think about and secondly, it's not strictly true. Certainly not for the two or three people sitting in their living room watching you – they think you're talking directly to them. It helps to visualise someone you know and place them in the lens of the camera – a friend or relative, perhaps. My advice is to use someone who you know likes you, wants you to do well, and is not critical or judgemental. Talk to them, tell them the story, invite them to watch, give them the news. You may find you need to change that friend for different programmes, maybe to an older friend, a colleague or even a child. For every programme, find a 'friend' who would be interested and then decide what your role is. Are you a teacher? A conduit for information? An entertainer? Above all, *talk to your viewer.*

'Treat the camera like it's someone you know. It's easy then to target the person you're talking to. I've got a friend I respect a lot, and often I talk to them. If it's City Hospital, I talk to my Mum or my Grandma.
Suzi Perry (Sky Sports, BBC City Hospital)

OPINIONS AND ATTITUDES

Consciously or subconsciously, the viewers will read your intentions and your feelings. They'll know whether you want to be in the studio, whether you are interested in the subject you are talking about, and how you regard your guests. They'll pick it up from your energy or your body language, your eye contact, vocal inflection and a hundred other seemingly small ways. Be careful to impart only those opinions and attitudes you intend to communicate. In most programmes it won't matter what those are; in fact, some producers want their presenters to be opinionated and even controversial. Check the programme remit. But there is one form of presenting that *must* remain unbiased – the news.

As a newsreader it's essential that you can be trusted. The viewer does not want your views or your emotions. You are a voice of authority and the viewer relies on you for honest information. This is covered in more detail in *Interviewing* (pp. 103-116).

WHAT THEY SAY

'I think that the people who are good presenters are natural, look confident, are pleasant to watch and invite your respect. You have to believe what you are being told and believe in the person who is telling you.'
Sophie Raworth (BBC Breakfast News)

'It's not all ego. If you can't get on with people or are not interested in them, then don't be a presenter. You have to want to communicate.'
Siân Lloyd (TV weather presenter)

'Each one of us is unique. Be honest. If it rings true for you, then do it. Trust your instincts.'
Matthew Kelly (Stars in Their Eyes, Game for a Laugh)

'I'm convinced that an audience warms to a presenter who shows some warmth, some humour and emotion when things are not so good, and tries to bring them in using fairly direct language.'
Huw Edwards (BBC News, 6 O'clock News, formerly Chief Correspondent for BBC News 24)

'Viewers like to see someone who is obviously comfortable with what they are doing, and feel that they will not be phased if some-

thing goes wrong. If there's a touch of humour or something about them, that to me is what the knack is.'
Simon McCoy (SKY News)

'You've got to be likeable – someone you wouldn't mind going for a drink with. It's more about communicating than just imparting information. It's projecting a warmth. Be genuinely enthusiastic, even if it's a relatively dull story.'
Kirsty Lang (Channel 4 News)

'A good presenter is someone who believes in what they are saying and doing, and who wants others to be as thrilled or excited as they are.'
Johnny Ball (Play School, Variety Show)

3

Visual Impact

It's generally accepted that the impact we make on others depends:

- 7–10% on what we say
- 38–40% on how something is said
- 50–55% on how we look and behave.

Have you ever made a judgement about a stranger within the first few minutes of meeting them? Most of us do this, whether consciously or subconsciously, all the time. It is an instinctive reaction: our innate survival responses are 'checking out' whether the newcomer can be trusted or not by making an initial visual search for mutual signs of agreement. Wearing clothing of a similar style may superficially identify you as part of the same team, and therefore as sharing similar views. Posture, gesture, eye contact, mannerisms, clothing, make-up and hair are all factors contributing to the way in which you will be perceived.

Television is a visual medium and without doubt the first impression that you give is lasting, so it is important that you get it right. In everyday introductions we have generally made a character assumption within the first four minutes of contact. In public speaking the audience will form an opinion within the first 30 seconds of the presentation. In television, it is within just *10 seconds* – that's all the time you get. It's not essential to be the most beautiful figure ever to appear on screen – in some instances that may even work against you – but the presentation of your image is vital.

'How you start a programme is so important. An audience can turn off very quickly if they don't like you for some reason. I always try to be very open and welcoming and I dress to match that feeling.'
Julie Peasgood (*BBC Pebble Mill, Children in Need*)

MATCH YOUR IMAGE AND YOUR PERSONALITY

Having explored and defined your personal style as a presenter – as discussed in the previous chapter – it can be very easy to undermine yourself by sending unintentional and conflicting messages via the visual image you create. For example, it would be difficult to take seriously a presenter of futuristic design concepts who wears dowdy clothes. So be sure that the whole picture is consistent. This is where professional advice comes into its own. Don't be afraid to approach colour and design consultants (and make-up artists, where applicable) for their advice and personal guidance. You can then ensure that your look suits your personality and style. As well as looking your best, enhancing your personal image results in increased self-confidence which, in turn, improves your performance.

EXERCISE

Look at yourself in a long mirror. What does your total image say about you? Look at your body. Look at the way you stand. Look at your hair, your clothing and accessories. Are you smart, tidy, uniform, fashionable, glamorous, casual?

From the list below, select 10 qualities that you consider currently reflect your image. Be honest – we're talking about your image *now*, not what you would like it to be. You may, if you wish, add two or three qualities that you feel are more appropriate to you but are not listed here.

Professional	Confident	Experienced	Innovative
Creative	Homely	Determined	Witty
Youth-orientated	Anarchic	Fun	Relaxed
Fashionable	Traditional	Knowledgeable	
Energetic	Friendly	Assertive	
Quirky	Encouraging	Down-to-earth	

Choose from your list the three qualities that are most dominant in your current image.

_____

_____

_____

How do these match up with the image of 'you, the presenter' that we identified in the previous chapter? As you read through this chapter, pick out the image elements that you think will enhance your style and presentation.

BODY LANGUAGE

Body language is the physical expression of thought. We may, for no apparent reason, feel at ease with someone we have just met; alternatively, we may 'sense' that something someone says does not ring true. We tend to put such responses down to 'intuition' or 'being perceptive', when in fact we are subconsciously reading a person's body language. Some signs are more obvious than others, such as folding the arms in front – an action that can be interpreted as defensive, showing an unwillingness to engage, or indicating disagreement with another. The simple action of rubbing the earlobe can indicate that a person has heard enough or wants to block out what they are hearing. Alternatively, open palms may demonstrate honesty and a willingness to listen.

Some telltale gestures are so small that only a television camera will pick them up. That tiny twitch of the lip, suggesting cynicism, or slow blink of the eyes indicating lying or recognition of a lie, can reveal your true thoughts. These mini-signals are more noticeable when you say one thing but your body language is saying something else . . . 'I completely agree with you,' says the presenter, whilst scratching the back of his neck – the action contradicting the speech. It would be a mistake, however, to read each individual gesture in isolation. If someone rubs their nose, it could be for several different reasons. Perhaps it's cold, or they have an itch or are about to sneeze – or perhaps they are indeed lying. Just as all languages are made up of a collection of words, phrases and sentences, so is body language made up of a mixture or cluster of signals. Interpreting body language can give you the upper hand as well as an insight into your own communication skills, but – although you should be conscious of the signals you are giving out – there is no need to become obsessive about every gesture. There are plenty of books devoted to this subject, some of which are listed in the Further Reading section at the back of this book.

Getting a response

Non-verbal communication can have a very strong effect on the response given by a viewer or interviewee. Used wisely, a slight change in posture can effectively produce an interesting interview. Many an unsuspecting interviewee has been more candid than they intended, when faced with an interviewer who understands the concept of body language. Likewise, an unco-operative interviewee may become more responsive to an interviewer who displays signals of encouragement, such as nodding sympathetically or slightly tilting the head to one side. The latter is particularly effective as an open and non-aggressive pose.

POSTURE

This is an essential element of a positive physical image. With good posture you can wear almost anything; with bad posture, even an Armani suit can look like a cheap imitation. Your posture gives you 'style'. Have you ever heard the expressions 'It's how you wear it', 'She'd look good in anything'? Stand up straight and be noticed.

Notice how people sit or stand when they present or interview. Take time to view your own posture at different times of the day. What image are you creating?

EXERCISE
How do you sit, walk, stand, listen? Try it out. Walk into a room, sit down, listen to someone talking or imagine someone is talking to you.

Practise with the radio or TV. Imagine that the presenter is in your room, sitting on your sofa, talking directly to you. Were you physically engaged in what you were doing? Were you presenting an image of someone who is interested and interesting?

As an important element of body language, your posture can say more about you than any clever scriptwriting. If you are over-relaxed with an 'I'm not interested, I couldn't be bothered' look, then why should the viewer pay attention? They'll turn off or change channels. Here are some more guidelines:

- If you're sitting or standing rigidly, bolt upright, then the viewer is likely to see you as officious, stern and perhaps even aloof and patronising.
- Rounded or hunched shoulders send messages of fear, defensiveness or low status. Try to keep your torso lifted and your shoulders open.
- When you are sitting, remain upright and make sure that your bottom is in the back of the chair. If it is a deep seat, sit forwards but

make sure that your back is straight. Slouching can indicate a lack of interest or arrogance.

- Leaning forwards and peering at the camera lens is considered intrusive. Imagine if someone was talking to you like that in your living room – you would tell them to 'back off'.
- If you do lean back, keep your chin up. As well as being a negative, defensive image, the studio lighting will give you 'double chins'.
- Steady, smooth arm movements give an air of authority.

EXERCISE
Turn down the sound on the television and note the body language and posture of presenter and interviewee. Select different types of programmes, such as daytime magazine-style shows, chat shows and current affairs programmes. See if you can guess what they are feeling.

What is a neutral posture?
Basically, a good, neutral posture involves standing up straight. It is very easy to adopt what you think is a comfortable posture that is, in fact, out of line. Try the following exercise and see how it feels.

EXERCISE
- Stand in front of a long mirror.
- Place your feet slightly apart, in line with your hips.
- Lean your weight very slightly forwards over the balls of your feet.
- Straighten your spine and be conscious of its length from your pelvis to your neck. Extend that feeling as though a piece of string were attached to the spine, running through to the top of your head and lifting you up.
- Release any tension from your neck by gently shaking your head from side to side as if saying *no*. Make sure your shoulders are down and relaxed. Giving them a little shrug may help. Relax your arms and hands down by your side.
- Take in a deep breath and, feeling as tall as possible, breathe out slowly without collapsing your body.

Some more tips on posture
Your body should always look as though it's filled with energy. You need to find the balance between relaxed and unfocused. You can be assertive, but not arrogant. You can even jump up and down as long as you remain natural and engaged in the process – but keep in the camera

frame! Control swivel chairs and be conscious of how much you twist and turn in them.

> 'Too much movement – head, shoulders and arms, swinging back in the chair – can make you look like you're on speed. It's amazing how distracting even the tiniest, irrelevant movement can be on TV.'
> *Jeremy Vine (BBC Newsnight)*

Be wary of slippery sofas and chairs. The designer may think that they look simply wonderful, but fail to take into account the fact that you, the presenter, have to sit on them. It's easy to over-relax in a huge chair, on a soft sofa or even on a bed, but you will lose your energy and more often than not just look uncomfortable. So sit up and engage.

Kirsty Lang (ITN Channel 4 News) was originally given a standard studio chair. She found it too big for her. If she sat back her feet didn't touch the floor, but if she sat forwards she was uncomfortably perched on the edge of the chair. 'The chair made me look and feel small in comparison to my male colleagues,' she explains. So she asked for a more suitable chair and a cushion to support her back so that she could sit up with ease.

Try not to make any sudden or sharp movements. If you do, it can be hard for the camera and the audience to keep up with you. Keep your body in slow motion and your mouth in gear! If your personal style is to be always on the move, find time to be still so that the viewer can register that it's you! Rehearse any new, inventive moves with the director so that when they cut to you, you are where you've agreed to be (or at the very least, the director, vision mixer and camera operator are aware that you may hop in and out of the shot).

Good posture is good for your voice. Poor posture can affect your vocal ability. If you are slumped over, you are bending the vocal instrument: breath support is restricted and vocal quality impaired. There is also a tendency to mumble, and then to start being lazy and disengage. You can start, finish in and go back to a neutral posture when you become aware that you are slouching, moving about too much or leaning.

WALKING

Walking and talking – things you do every day without so much as a passing thought. But suddenly the cameras are focused on you and you become an alien invader from a sci-fi B movie. Your speech slows down. You take over-long, careful strides with your elbows glued to your sides as your hands flap and twitch.

Instead, *be natural*. It's easy, you do it every day. Try it now.

EXERCISES
(1) Walk around the room reciting a nursery rhyme, poem or any ditty you know well. Do the same on a given topic – e.g. lunch menu, journey to work, how to play tennis.
(2) Imagine a line drawn horizontally along the wall. Focusing along the line, walk across the room, again reciting a nursery rhyme, poem or any ditty you know well. *Relax*. Do the same on a given topic, as before (lunch menu, journey to work, how to play tennis).
(3) Now be daring and speak your opening lines! 'Hello, my name is .... and welcome to my bathroom.'

FEET

When you stand, is your weight evenly distributed? Do you lean on one foot and perhaps ballet dance with the other? Do you shuffle from one foot to the other?

When sitting, especially with your legs crossed, do your feet remain still? Perching on the edge of a desk has become a familiar pose. It looks great if you keep your back straight and hold your position; the dangerous tendency is to swing your legs or waggle your feet. Fine, if that's what you intend to do, but remember that it can be distracting – and what body language signals are you sending out?

If your feet are going to be in shot, what are your shoes like? Are they polished, clean, heeled and soled properly? What do they say about you? Make sure that you feel comfortable in your shoes, especially if you are wearing them all day and, more particularly, if you are walking in vision. Stilettos are not always welcome in the studio, because they mark the floor.

Socks and tights

Whilst we're talking about feet, let's take a look at the socks you wear. Keeping in mind your image, choose the colour, pattern and length wisely. Make sure they come up over your calves. A flash of flesh between the ankle sock and trouser turn-up is not attractive. Novelty socks may not be suitable for a serious, corporate image. Bright colours distract.

Ladies should wear tights or stockings. Bare legs, no matter how beautiful they are, look blotchy under studio lights (and often in need of support). This does not necessarily apply to outside broadcasts (OB), but judge for yourself whether conditions demand that you wear them or not. For the sake of presentation check that their colour and condition is of the best.

HANDS

What do you do with them? This is the perennial question asked by so many presenters. After-dinner speakers, corporate conference presenters, TV presenters and even actors suddenly find that their hands feel as if they don't belong to them. It's easy to say, 'Just forget about them,' but generally the more you try to forget them the larger they seem to get.

'I was so excitable I talked with my hands, which obviously distracts the viewer, because your hands are waving around like you've got the chequered flag and no-one listens to what you're saying. So I practised for a couple of hours a day talking and sitting on my hands.'
Kevin Duala (BBC Holiday Programme)

First of all, identify what you do with your hands. Do you wring them in anxiety, clasp them tightly in front of you, fiddle with your jacket, stroke your head, or flap them about as if signing in semaphore or swatting flies? Recognise your habitual mannerisms. Ask someone to watch you. If it's not distracting, then it won't matter what you do with your hands as long as you keep all gestures as part of a natural movement and not as a nervous habit. However, don't put your hand in front of your mouth: it's bad body language and restricts vocal delivery. Find a resting place where you can put your hands if you feel they are beginning to wander. Here are some suggestions.

- Let your arms and hands hang loosely by your side. Take care not to let your fingers twitch.
- If you put your hands in your pockets, make sure that you keep them still.
- Hold a script or clipboard, but be careful not to use it as a shield between you and the audience or to grip it with white-knuckle tension.

- Fold one hand into the other lightly and hold them close to your tummy, at hip height.
- If you are sitting, fold both hands together and place them on your lap.
- You may be fortunate enough to have a desk in front of you on which you can rest your hands with your fingers lightly interlocked. Keep them still and don't be tempted to fiddle with a pen.

Try different positions for yourself, and choose the most comfortable. Once you do this you can then concentrate fully on your script or presentation and your gestures will quite naturally support your intentions. Be positive.

Always make sure that your hands are clean and that your nails are manicured (men too), especially if you are demonstrating in close-up. (Exceptions can be made for the DIY expert or gardener – a little bit of dirt and hard skin can add to your credibility.) Do you wear rings? If so, how many and do they distract? Do you wear nail varnish? Does the colour distract? It is better not to wear any at all than to present on camera with bits of colour chipped off the varnish.

EYES

Eyeline and eye contact

When you are talking directly to the camera it is very important that you hold eye contact. TV presenter Matthew Kelly is in total agreement. 'Talk to one person at a time when you talk to the camera. Don't ever think that you're talking to 5 million. Imagine you are just speaking as I'm speaking to you now. This is absolutely crucial.' Kirsty Lang (Channel 4 News) says, 'My advice is always to talk to just one person. Explain a news item as if you were talking to a friend.'

Always talk to the camera lens. Not above, below or to either side of it. If you watch a programme with two presenters, you will notice how when one presenter is talking to camera, the co-presenter often also looks directly at the camera with the occasional glance to their colleague. This sends messages to the viewer of confidence and reassurance. It doubles the level of conviction and authority and tells the viewer that the presenters are working from the same script, literally and metaphorically. Keep your head still with no jerky, shifty or sharp movements, and keep your eyes open.

Spectacles

If you're not happy wearing contact lenses, then don't. There is no reason why you shouldn't wear spectacles: in fact, some people consider a bespectacled presenter to have specialist knowledge or to be an expert of some sort. The important point here is that the viewer should still see your eyes. Keep your glasses on the bridge of your nose; if they slip down, apart from being irritating to you, they will mask your eyes. For the same reason – this time because the lights are so bright – try to find anti-glare or non-reflective lenses. Tinted glasses should be avoided because they restrict eye contact.

Select frames which complement your features as well as your personality. The right shape or colour can instantly improve your image. Frames should be no lower than the centre of your cheeks or wider than the face. The general advice is to avoid shapes that duplicate that of your face. If you have sharp features, wear softer-shaped frames or, if you have a round face, choose a frame that is more angular. Here are some basic guidelines:

Face Shape	Frames
Square	High-sided frames. Narrow frames. Soft angles
Round	High-sided frames. Strong, angled frames to give definition and draw attention to the cheekbones
Rectangular	Narrow frames with a deep shape. Soft angles to soften the bone structure
Oval	Almost any shape. Nothing too dominant

HAIR

Hair should always be clean and tidy with a styled cut. Again, it's important to make sure that your eyes are visible; a long fringe, or hair hanging loosely at the side of your face, can throw shadows and prevent a clear image of you. Kirsty Lang says, 'I got letters from viewers saying that I should get rid of my fringe. Then an editor told me to get it cut as it looked as if my hair was in my eyes and it was very distracting.' TV presenter Debbie Greenwood once had very long hair: 'It looked different on screen than in real life; it caused all sorts of shadows and looked very flat. I changed to having a hair *style* rather than just long hair hanging loose. I also brushed it back off my face.'

According to one hair stylist, if you want your hair to have that rough-dried look, be prepared to spend an hour or so blow drying it – otherwise it will just look a mess with no style at all. Presentation takes time, which (according to ITN news) is why more women presenters are having their hair cut short! Spray or gel flyaway hair. This applies to both men and women, but don't overdo it. You want it to stay in place, not to look set in iron. Be aware that studio lighting has a flattening effect on hair: that doesn't mean you should backcomb it into a beehive, just bear the effect in mind and make a slight adjustment to your style if you need to.

If you are outside it is particularly important that the wind doesn't blow your hair over your face or make it stand up on end. It's not always possible to find a location out of the wind, so think ahead before you go out. You might consider tying or pinning back long hair, or using a fixing gel or spray to avoid an untidy look or distracting image.

Highlights
If you have highlights or colour, get the roots attended to regularly to avoid that dark regrowth which is emphasised under the lights.

Dandruff
Try to rectify the problem with the appropriate shampoo. Brush jacket shoulders and lapels as regularly as possible. You may consider wearing a lighter coloured suit or top.

Receding hairline
This isn't a problem in itself, but in studio locations do ensure that you make up to the hair roots and powder your scalp so that it doesn't shine!

Hair-pieces
How many times have you noticed someone on television with a hair-piece and said, 'That's a wig'? If you do choose to wear one it had better be good, and be aware of adverse weather conditions during outside broadcasts.

Clean shave or beard?
To shave or not to shave is a decision for you and your producer. It will depend on your programme and your own style as a presenter. If you have a beard, keep it clean and trimmed. If you don't have a strong jawline, a closely cropped beard can actually help to create definition. From the point of view of presentation, the less you hide your face, the more communication you have with the viewer.

'I bought into the idea of acceptability. I used to be pretty outrageous, now I'm more middle of the road. You've got to get the audience to accept you in the first place; you don't want to lose them before you start. I trimmed my beard.'
Matthew Kelly (Stars in Their Eyes, Game for a Laugh)

Eyebrows

Properly shaped eyebrows can enhance your eyes and be very attractive. Attend to wayward hairs, trim and pluck them accordingly. Too thinly trimmed and your eyes will seem to stare; too fair and you'll need to shade them carefully with an eyebrow pencil. The 'one eyebrow, fuzzy caterpillar' look is unattractive and definitely distracting. Separate and define, and most definitely see a beauty specialist – don't shave them!

Hairy ears and nostrils

Do the decent thing, cut or pluck them.

TEETH

I believe that cosmetic dental surgery should only be considered if your teeth inhibit clear speech or if their appearance makes you so self-conscious that you cannot present with ease. If you have the option, choose white fillings to match the colour of your teeth. Chipped or crooked teeth can often be capped with white porcelain crowns. Some presenters have their teeth whitened on a regular basis. Whatever you choose to do, keep them clean. Always check before a recording or transmission that there is no tiny piece of spinach or fruit seed from lunch still lodged between your teeth! Likewise, watch for any traces of lipstick. The camera operator or director may not notice it until it is too late. It really is up to you.

MAKE-UP AND CLOTHES

Whilst the majority of the following image tips apply to both sexes, not everything applies to everyone. The main point you need to remember is that anything that can distract the viewers' attention, will. Decide who's going to be the star of the show. Will it be your hands, your hair, your fluorescent shirt or you?

In most studios there will be someone around to advise you. On major shows there will be a designer, a wardrobe supervisor and a make-up artist. But the smaller the budget, the more the producer will rely on you to look after yourself, and in the corporate world you are more often than not left to your own devices. If you are unsure of how something looks on screen, *always* ask. It's much better to check whether a colour or pattern works before the recording than to leave it and regret it afterwards. So, beginning with make-up, here are some basics.

MAKE-UP

Skin

Everyone needs to wear a base foundation when filming or recording in the studio – this is not just true of TV studios, but wherever an indoor studio set is constructed (an office, a boardroom, a bar or a lounge). TV presenter Paul Coia initially refused to wear make-up, apparently preserving his male dignity. 'But I soon changed my mind when I saw how pale and washed-out I looked. It didn't matter what I looked like for radio, but it did for TV. You have to make an effort.'

The studio lights, wherever they are erected, will bleach the colour from your skin. If you are unused to putting on make-up or unsure which colours to use, seek advice from a professional make-up artist. Try a shade deeper than your normal skin tone. Apply with a small, damp cosmetic sponge and blend in carefully, leaving no block lines. Use the foundation sparingly and then use a neutral face powder to set the foundation – this prevents the make-up from sweating off, and reduces any shine. There are all-in-one foundation and powder products on the market which do a fantastic job and are well worth investigating.

The studio lights also have a tendency to flatten out facial features, so you may need to use a blusher or contour shading. Avoid any sparkle or super-shine which will catch the light and make you look hot and sweaty. Check in the camera monitor or with a make-up artist. Cover blemishes with make-up concealer. *Always* use powder. You may need to 'touch up' several times during the course of your time in the studio as it can get quite hot under the lights. Very often the floor manager or the director will let you know if you are 'shining', or you can always ask them if you are and then take the necessary action.

Eyes

Decide whether or not you need to define your eye shape. For men, a little mascara may be all that's needed. Women should at least put on the basics. However, unless the style of programme or your personal style requires it, keep the look natural. Use nothing that sparkles unless you're making a fashion statement.

Lips

Some people have very dry lips and long hours in the studio can cause dehydration, so moisturise using a lip salve or chapstick. Lipstick is often just as effective, especially if it already has a moisturising ingredient. The colour of lipstick you wear will depend on your skin tone and your clothes, but the general guidelines are:

- outline lips with a lip pencil to give definition
- too pale gives a washed-out appearance
- too bright can look 'tarty' and worse, can *move* on the screen
- keep the gloss effect down to a minimum
- only use enough to coat your lips lightly and naturally.

CLOTHES

The bad news is that TV makes you look 5–10 lb heavier on screen. The good news is that by wearing the right clothing you can lessen the effect. If you are slim you can still benefit from choosing the right clothes to make the most of your shape and figure.

Do your clothes fit?

Do your clothes actually fit?
Whatever you wear it's essential that you feel comfortable and that your clothes fit you well. You don't want to be worrying whether your sleeves are riding up your arms, your trousers are too tight, or your jacket is slipping off your shoulders. It doesn't matter how impressive the label is, if a garment doesn't fit properly it won't give you style or make you look good. Do the buttons fasten without pulling? Can you move and gesture with ease? Err on the side of close-fitting, rather than the baggy look to given a clean, sharp finish.

Do your clothes fit your image and identity?
You will feel more at ease if your clothing matches your own style and personality. However, it may be that the producer or designer will have their own ideas about the visual image of the programme and will want you to conform to the overall picture.

Do your clothes fit and complement the programme?
Wear what is appropriate to the programme and its style. At times it might be important to reflect a national mood, i.e. a state funeral. Use your discretion.

The response you get during an interview may be influenced by body language *and* by what you're wearing. It has been known for a journalist to be refused an interview because they were inappropriately dressed. This applies particularly if you are working abroad. Be sensitive to the conditions around you and the accepted dress code. Use your judgement.

The interviewer and comedian Mark Thomas not only relies on his persuasive personal manner but alters his body language and style of clothing to get the interview he wants. Often his subjects are wooed into thinking that he is supportive and non-threatening, when his investigative intent is far more probing. He then changes into more comfortable clothing to present his show in his own natural style.

Newsreaders should keep it smart and simple. You are the bearer of good and bad tidings.

'Be smart but not distracting. Your clothes should be nicely cut. They should enhance but not distract from what you are saying.'
Sophie Raworth (BBC News)

EXERCISE
Watch presenters and study what they wear. What can you 'read' from their clothing? As you hop across the TV channels you'll soon be aware that almost anything goes, but judge for yourself what works well and what doesn't.

Look at the presenters whom you admire. Look at the programmes you identify with and the type of programme you would like to present. Does the presenter visually match the programme content and style? Is there anything that makes the presenter look special?

Mic and earpiece packs
These small boxes are generally clipped on to a belt, tucked into a pocket or put in a pouch on an elastic waistband. The small of the back is the most natural and safest place for them to be. Great effort used to be made to hide them under clothing, but now it's deemed unimportant if the viewer sees them. The batteries in these transmitters can die very quickly, no matter how new they are, so it's essential that access to mic and earpiece packs is as trouble-free as possible. Be aware of this when you choose what to wear.

What to wear

Juggling what fits well with what feels right, and with what is appropriate to the programme remit, can give you a serious headache – especially on a day-to-day basis. When it comes down to it, what you wear has to balance all the factors and still retain an element of personal choice.

Patterns

From a visual point of view, if you are small or petite big patterns can overpower you and make you look even smaller. Fancy patterns can be distracting. Try not to wear anything too busy. Closely spaced, thin, narrow lines tend to strobe on screen, as do checks and finely woven tweeds.

Colours

Colour is a powerful image tool. In the natural world every colour has a message and purpose, and an element of that exists in our everyday visual perception. On a practical level some colours work fantastically well on certain presenters and yet the same colour can make another presenter look pale and washed-out. Generally, bright, saturated colours work well on screen, but get advice from a colour consultant or a designer. It's a good idea to have a small selection of tops and jackets to give the director and producer a choice. If you are unsure whether the colour or pattern of a garment will be suitable, take it into the studio and hold it up within the camera sight and in front of the set you will be working on. Use a monitor to see for yourself what it looks like. Take a look at the set design, chairs, furniture and the colour of the backing flats and choose a different tone or colour to wear. You don't want to disappear. And, speaking of disappearing, will you be working in front of any chroma key screens? Check the colour of any screens and flats being used. They are usually painted blue or green, which are the colours most distant from the skin's natural tones. If you wear the same colour as the chroma key screen, the projected image will appear straight through you. This is covered in more detail on pp. 117-22. In general, be wary of these colours and pigments:

- *White*: can flare on screen and distract. With high-quality camera and transmission equipment it's less likely to happen; nevertheless, white can dominate the picture. It's fine to wear it at the neckline of a shirt, blouse or tee-shirt, but try not to wear it as your main colour.
- *Black*: absorbs light and flattens the whole look of the garment, reducing any shape or definition. You can slightly reduce this impres-

sion by choosing a textured fabric such as velvet or a silk with an embossed pattern. Again, try it out in front of the camera if you are at all unsure.

- *Red*: sometimes this colour can work well, but you have to be careful which shade of red you wear. A poppy red can seem to 'move' on the screen – you will notice a fuzzy blur on the outlining edge. A browny red is a better shade and looks very good on camera. You may also consider wearing a red with a pattern on it which will break up the solid block of colour.

Ties

The following is a light-hearted look at tie patterns and what they can 'say' about you. Of course, personal preference will always come into play – but if you're in doubt as to the appropriateness or otherwise of your choice, check with a professional.

Pattern	Visual Interpretation
Plain	Neutral but dependent on the colour. Generally it says style and someone not wanting to give too much away
Plain with a single motif	Implies power and influence. Suggests wearer is a member of a club or desires to be part of a group. Could be inflexible
Diagonal stripes	Respectable, traditional, trustworthy. The bolder and wider the stripe, the more outgoing the wearer. (*Note*: lots of thin stripes can strobe on screen)
Small spots	Widely spaced spots indicate reliability and independence. Lots of small spots suggest an introvert who prefers to work with others
Large spots	The wearer may be brash and forceful. Has a sense of humour but you had better like their jokes!
Checks	Likes order and conformity. Could be controlling. Large checks indicate ambition, smaller checks indicate attention to detail. (*Note*: tiny, woven checks can strobe on screen)
Paisley	A traditionalist with an ability to depart from the norm, without being confrontational
Geometric designs	Creative and practical
Floral designs	Sensitive and approachable
Jokey	A fun-loving person, or would like to be!

Jon Snow wears bright ties to 'cheer things up a bit'. Whatever your preference, choose good-quality ties with a good lining. Balance the width of tie with the width of your lapels. Slightly-built figures tend to be overwhelmed by bolder tie patterns, whereas a small knotted tie might look a bit silly on someone bigger.

Jewellery

Avoid anything that is likely to distract the viewers' attention from your face. Brooches and badges worn on the lapel or around the neckline bring the viewers' focus in towards the centre of the picture. Select items that complement the shape of your face. Shiny brooches and garish rings can reflect and dazzle in the studio lights. Make sure that nothing you wear is noisy, such as bracelets and earrings that jangle. Avoid pendants and necklaces that hang down close to a clip-on microphone; the viewer wants to hear you, not the rattle and thump of your accessories.

MAKING THE MOST OF YOUR BODY SHAPE

If there is any area of your body which you would rather not draw attention to – 'a problem area' – then keep clothes simple at that point. Elaborate attempts to camouflage it with extra colours or accessories will only attract attention. Try to draw the eye away from the area you don't want to emphasise. In fact, a television presenter's main consideration should be to draw attention to the face, the focal point of communication. Aim for neatness around the neck, since any fuss in this area will distract the attention from your face. Always wear the correct collar size. The following information is by no means a definitive guide but a generalised and useful overview.

EXERCISE

Stand back from the mirror. Look at yourself from a distance, as if on a long shot. Take a good look at your body shape. Is it angular, pear-shaped, rounded, petite, stocky? Are your shoulders broad, sloping, narrow? Walk towards the mirror and see yourself as if in a mid-shot. Look at your face shape and your neck. Have you a round or oval face? Is your neck long or short?

Choosing shapes

Select a collar shape and neckline to suit the shape of your face. The guiding rule is not to emphasise or 'repeat' your features. For example, if you have a curved, round face then it's best to avoid high, round necklines, high collars and softer-edged lapels. Try choosing V-necks, dropped necklines and pointed collars.

Choose a neckline to compliment your neck shape. If you have double chins or a short or thick neck, avoid high polo-neck sweaters and any fussy chains. Likewise, a long, thin neck will look better on TV if you avoid long V-necks and collarless shirts.

It's just as important to be conscious of what you wear below the waist, especially for long-framed shots. Whilst comfort is a priority, make sure that bigger tummies are covered and not supported underneath by a belt or waistband. Avoid wide belts and short jackets and any detail on the hips or waistline. On TV, short legs don't look good in wide trousers, long jackets or full skirts. It's preferable to stick to shorter jackets, and choose one colour or tones of the same colour.

Skirt lengths
- Unless you have gorgeous legs, keep away from the pelmet length skirt.
- When you are sitting down, tight skirts tend to ride up your thighs and reveal more than you might wish. It can be distracting if you start pulling your skirt down. And if that isn't enough, when you sit down, thighs flatten and spread out.

EXERCISE
Prepare one of the following items which you can present to camera. Wear what you consider appropriate.

- Introduce yourself, say your name, describe where you live. Talk about your occupation, subjects studied or favourite hobby.
- Describe why you want to be a TV presenter.
- Present a report on a local event. Choose something from your local paper or an event you have seen or know about.

Video yourself making this presentation. Review it, be your own critic. Make notes on posture, body language, gesture, facial expression and a head-to-toe visual impact analysis.

IN SUMMARY

- Take a good look at your visual impact.
- Check your body language.
- Posture – sit, stand or walk with poise and attention.
- Mannerisms and gestures should be within the camera frame and in your control.

- Strive to be natural and engaged in the process.
- Wear clothes which are appropriate to the programme style and your personal image – and which are comfortable.
- Choose clothes with a good cut that flatter your shape.
- Check that colours and patterns don't distract.
- Aim for neatness around the neckline.
- Wear the correct collar size.
- Ensure that jewellery doesn't distract or jangle.
- Hair should be clean and styled.
- Shoes should be clean and suitable.
- Wear make-up. Powder at regular intervals.
- Glasses should be non-reflective, compatible with your image and the shape of your face, and not tinted.
- If in any doubt, check with your producer or director.

Finally, whatever you wear, here are two absolutes.

(1) Be sure to turn off all mobile phones, pagers, watch alarms and personal organisers. Silence anything electrical that is likely to bleep or ring when you least want it to.

(2) Empty pockets of loose change and keys. They may rattle, fall out onto the floor or you may be tempted to play with them nervously in your pocket. Don't. It's better to leave them in your dressing room or with your other valuables and personal effects.

WHAT THEY SAY

'I tried to find something I liked about myself. I like my smile, but then I never really smiled! When I got given a show I thought, "How am I going to relax?" The only way to make your face relax is to smile.'
Trevor Nelson (MTV, BBC Radio 1)

'I had always been used to the video camera at home, but when you see yourself on TV for the first time you see things you don't like. I thought my hair was too dark and heavy so I put slices of colour through it; it looks better textured now. Also, the weight thing. The camera definitely adds on weight. Watch out for dark circles under your eyes when you've been working hard.'
Suzi Perry (Sky Sports, BBC City Hospital)

'Weather comes at the end of the news. It's factual and that reflects on what we wear. I like smart jackets, I always have – and it's amazing how a simple piece of jewellery can give life to an old jacket. We are restricted by colours and patterns and so forth because of technical requirements, as well as budget.'
Siân Lloyd (TV weather presenter)

'I certainly take more notice of what I look like now. People always mention what I wear. I try to keep up with fashion and styles as well as choosing a style I'm happy with. You can't just wear a pair of old trackie bottoms! I turned up one day looking really bad and it was just my luck that I was asked to do a line-up test for a new producer. The one day you don't bother, that's the day they call on you or you bump into someone important.'
Kate MacIntyre (Channel 5)

'The first couple of minutes is absolutely crucial in creating impact. Visual image is terrifyingly important, and anyone who disagrees simply doesn't understand the impact of the screen in people's homes. People who don't pay attention to it will reap a very bitter harvest, so it's worth investing in it. The biggest change for me was that I stopped wearing spectacles. It's not a golden rule; some people can wear them and look good – but they have to be very good. And being a correspondent is very different from anchoring the show every night. The focus is on you: clothes, hair, style, weight. You have to be brutally honest with yourself and take good advice.'
Huw Edwards (BBC 6 O'Clock News)

'I cut my hair shorter, as it is neater for the studio. There is a strong influence from producers and focus groups. I saw a stylist, but most of their advice was unsuitable for straight news – the pink satin number wouldn't work! Ultimately, you are responsible for your own image. Watch your own tape and have an idea what looks good for you. Judge the light. Channel 4 lights are quite subtle and too much make-up doesn't work. Framing is important and being in a comfortable chair, feet on the floor and rooted, adds to security.'
Kirsty Lang (Channel 4 News)

4

Using Your Voice Effectively

As a TV presenter, you need to use your voice effectively. Because it is distilled over the airwaves, and because you are being heard from a box across a room, you need to give a little bit more volume, a touch clearer diction and more variation and inflection than usual. Recognising your vocal characteristics are important if you want to make any changes or improve your delivery. I don't believe that anyone should try to change their voice by removing natural accents and dialects, unless of course they can't be understood – and that rarely happens. Accents are considered a positive plus in television today, so with such a variety of sounds, clarity in tone and diction are an absolute must.

> 'Like all pronounced accents, tone and diction have to be refined a little for network broadcasting. Anyone involved in broadcasting should take care to pronounce and enunciate clearly. Some of the heavier accents are not so fashionable: you can't ask the audience to struggle through an accent to understand what you are saying.'
> *Huw Edwards (BBC 6 O'Clock News)*

Voice and speech problems fall into three categories:

- organic, structural defects
- restrictions due to emotional, psychological or environmental factors
- misuse.

The first two categories will require help from speech therapists and associated professionals. The third – misuse – is something for which you can take personal responsibility, since it can benefit from the effort of exercise. If you have any problems with your voice or are in any doubt about how to practise, consult a professional voice coach. They can give you personal guidance and tuition, identifying the causes of strain and suggesting specific exercises that may improve areas of weakness. There are also many publications on voice production, some of which are listed at the back of this book (*see* p. 199). Because the whole vocal mechanism is such a delicate instrument – and an essential ingredient in good communication – it's very important that you take care of it. Keeping it healthy and in working order will keep you employed.

HOW IS SOUND PRODUCED?

Without too much technical detail, here are the basics of how the vocal mechanism works.

First of all, the rib-cage moves outwards and breath is taken into the lungs (inhaled). The diaphragm (a dome-shaped muscle dividing the thorax and the stomach) is drawn down and outwards, flattening to create more space for the lungs to expand. As you breathe out (exhale), so the air is driven out up through the trachea (the windpipe), up into the larynx (the voice box), then out through the mouth. The larynx, which is made up of cartilages, houses the epiglottis and the vocal cords; part of the larynx sticks out, forming the 'Adam's Apple'. The epiglottis is a stiff flap which allows air to pass in and out of the windpipe but covers it when you are swallowing, to ensure that food or drink passes down the oesophagus (food pipe) and thus preventing choking.

The vocal cords are more accurately described as two pale folds of tissue membrane, rather than 'cords', which suggests a string-like texture. They are responsible for making the sound of the voice. Normally, air passes silently through the narrow gap between the vocal cords (folds), but when they are pulled tight by muscles in the larynx, the cords vibrate with the air passing through and make sound.

EXERCISE
Put the flat of your hand on the front of your throat. Take in a breath through the mouth and let it out silently through the mouth. Take in another breath through the mouth and this time let the breath out on a voiced AH. You will feel the muscles tighten and the larynx vibrate.

TAKING CARE OF YOUR VOICE

The length and density of the vocal cords determine the pitch of the voice. Generally men have longer, thicker cords and therefore a deeper, lower voice. Women tend to have shorter and thinner cords and therefore produce a lighter sound. These delicate cords are easily bruised by over-work or shouting, or when they become dry. When damaged the vocal cords do not meet smoothly; the sound is rough or broken and in extreme cases there is no sound at all. Once damaged, the vocal cords can take several days or weeks to repair. There's little you can do about a dry atmosphere, and most studios are very dry, but you can help yourself by drinking lots of water to stop dehydration. If you are tired or have been shouting then you'll need to rest your voice. However, you can prevent a lot of damage by doing some gentle exercises *before* you start work. Maintaining good health and keeping fit both contribute to a good-sounding voice and consistency of tone. A presenter needs a healthy, clear voice!

Voice-care tips

- Drink lots of water.
- Hum regularly to keep the vocal mechanism exercised.
- Roll and shrug your shoulders to release tension.
- Avoid milky or sugary products.
- Stop smoking, it's very drying.
- When the weather is cold, keep your neck warm by wearing a scarf or polo-neck top.
- Take extra-special care if you have to work when you are suffering with a cold or sore throat.
- Coughing is a very harsh action on the throat and can cause damage whilst you are attempting to clear your throat. It's better to swallow and, if you must cough, do so very gently and with your mouth closed.

BREATHING AND POSTURE FOR THE VOICE

The previous chapter covered posture in relation to body language and image, but it is just as important to maintain a good posture for voice. Quite simply if you let your chest collapse, round your shoulders and drop your head it becomes difficult to take in enough breath to support your voice. Breath is the fuel of the voice. In everyday speech we tend to speak in short phrases which require only a small intake of breath. But it may be that your script – especially a voice-over script – will incorporate longer sentences requiring more breath, or lots of short phrases which you have to speak very quickly, giving you little time to snatch a breath in between. Using more inflection and speaking at a slower and clearer pace also requires more breath control. It's important, then, that you not only increase your ability to take in more breath, but also learn to control it so that it doesn't run out when you most need it. Breath also gives power to your voice; more breath is required to speak louder. A constant stream of breath produces a good tone, just as petrol feeds an engine. Exhaling too much breath makes the voice sound weak. Presenter Debbie Greenwood explains that she once sounded breathy and spoke in a high voice. She put this down to nerves (*see* also *Fighting Fears*, pp. 45-51). By practising some breathing exercises she not only managed to cope with her nerves but also increased the resonance in her voice. Remain internally calm and *breathe*.

EXERCISES
(1) Shrug your shoulders up and down.
(2) Breathe in through your nose for a slow count of 3, and breathe out through the mouth slowly for a count of 3. Do this 5 times, keeping your shoulders down.
(3) Breathe in and reach forwards with your arms, lifting them up above your head. Stretch your fingers and as you breathe out, release your arms out to the side – bringing them slowly down to a count of 10. Breathe in, raise your arms up at the side and stretch them up above your head. Breathe in and release them forwards and down, to a count of 10. Repeat.

QUALITY OF SOUND

A good sound is perceived to be one that is open and free from any restriction. It is a pleasant tone as opposed to a noise, and is often described as full and rich. Personality and individuality can be expressed with ease when the voice is free from tension. It should be stressed that a resonant sound can be made irrespective of dialect and accent – indeed, some voices are enhanced by regional melody and lilt.

Sound is made by vibration, and the bigger the space the sound has in which to vibrate, the more resonant the quality will be. This doesn't mean that you have to be the size of a house to have a rich voice. What you do need to do is breathe more deeply and relax. Although the sound is created in the larynx you can use your upper torso as a resonating box, much the same as a double bass. If the body, shoulder and neck muscles are tight and tense, the space for sound to work in is limited. Relaxation exercises will help you (*see* also *Fighting Fears*, pp. 45-51) and remember to breathe deeply. Using the humming exercise below, you will feel the vibration in your chest, shoulders, neck and face. Gentle humming warms and tones the voice.

EXERCISES

(1) With your eyes closed, take a breath and very gently start to hum on a note you feel comfortable with.
HUMMMMMMMMMMM
Be careful not to force or push the sound, and try not to tighten your lips and jaw. Focus the sound in your mouth, cheekbones, nose, neck, shoulders and chest.
Keep taking breaths and humming until you can really feel the sound vibrating inside you.

(2) Hum a tune you know, preferably a ballad. Hum very gently and enjoy all the notes.

VOCAL VARIETY AND USING YOUR RANGE

In normal speech we use only a few notes of our range. Listen carefully to voices on TV and radio commercials. You'll hear energetic and lively voices as well as soft and gentle sounds, using a whole variety of notes. If you practise exercises using the whole of your range then it becomes more natural to use a wider range in everyday speech. As a result, you will make your voice more interesting to listen to.

EXERCISES

(1) Take a breath and hum on a comfortable centre note, and then hum on a descending slide. Go as low as you can. Take a breath and hum on an ascending slide. Go as high as you can. Gently hum up and down. Throughout, try to keep the voice full of resonance.

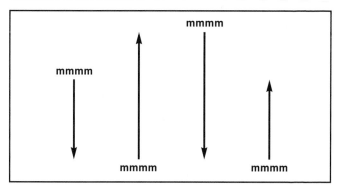

(2) Using the same exercise, slowly count to 5 down the slide and slowly count to 5 up the slide.

```
1        ↑  5
2        │  4
3        │  3
4        │  2
↓ 5      │  1
```

Lengthen the slide to increase the range of notes you can reach. Each time you practise this exercise start on a higher note and end on a lower note. Slowly your voice will find new, richer sounding notes in your range, giving you a greater vocal choice.

IT'S NOT WHAT YOU SAY, IT'S HOW YOU SAY IT

The voice can be so sensitive that it can be very difficult to disguise true feelings. For instance, when someone is holding back tears you can hear the strain in the voice – they are often described as 'choking with emotion'. Ideally, a skilled presenter should be the master of their own voice, recognising how and when to use it effectively. Having an ability to access a variety of notes and inflections gives you a greater freedom to express how you feel or how to convey an opinion – or, alternatively to detach yourself from an emotive subject so that you can present the facts without bias. In general, don't be afraid of colouring descriptive words. You can stress the difference between a small outbreak of cholera and a massive outbreak, or the difference between a beautiful design and a hideous concept. If you are given an assignment to climb to the top of a tower and the view is magnificent, it is not enough to speak decorous words, they need to be imbued with energy and feeling. If you are in a studio it can be more difficult, in which case try visualising what it is you are talking about. It will help to give credibility to what you say.

'Think about what you are reading, and visualise it – without being too dramatic. Too often people make the mistake of just reading a stack of words.'
Kirsty Lang (*Channel 4 News*)

Of course, how much expression you use will depend on the nature of your programme. It may be that for current affairs, news, documentary evidence or factual explanations you will need to detach yourself from your emotions. However, there is no reason for your delivery to be lifeless. Vocal variety is still important but it's a matter of judgement as to how far you can go. Detachment is a *general* rule but it is something you, as a responsible presenter, must be able to achieve.

ENERGY

Energy is the key to variety, but so too is a genuine interest in what you're saying. If you're bored with an item then the viewer will be too. They can just as easily get caught up in your apathy as they can in your enthusiasm.

'Thank you for coming on the show.' A simple and well-used phrase, but without energy or conviction it can sound as if the presenter couldn't care less whether the guest was there or not. It can happen quite unintentionally: the presenter may already be thinking about the next item and internally have moved on. It's such an easy habit to get into, but one to be avoided. Physically and vocally, keep your energy up.

EXERCISES
(1) Try saying the following phrases *without energy* and then *with energy*:

> 'It's one of the best hotels on the island.'
> 'A fact which causes everyone concern.'
> 'Dung Beetle are currently racing up the charts.'
> 'Good morning.'

Record yourself and play back your efforts. Note any differences.

(2) If you have a list to read out, remember that each item on the list has value. Perhaps not equal value, but importance just the same. Don't just recite a string of words – try using different inflections, pauses and emphases to vary your read. Visualising each item will help, too.

> 'The tour will include Greenwich Maritime Museum, St Paul's Cathedral, Leicester Square, Buckingham Palace and Regents Park.'
> 'The event includes tennis, cricket, rugby, soccer, snooker, ice hockey and bowls.'
> 'Tonight the contestants will attempt to make jam roly poly, a raspberry meringue nest, a lemon syllabub and a knickerbocker glory.'

VOLUME

Find a balance between speaking very softly and intimately, and shouting. Each programme will require a different vocal approach and attack, but don't make it difficult for the viewer to hear you. Your intention is to give information – and in any case, you will have a microphone. No one likes to be shouted at, even if you are on a Formula One race track. A noisy environment or high-energy show will necessarily require an increase in volume, especially if there is audience participation, but remember your friend in the camera lens. It's a matter of internal energy and a real desire to communicate. As a voice gets louder it can become harsh sounding and higher in pitch.

EXERCISE
(1)   Call out a list of instructions that you might hear in a game
         show. Remember to use breath support, relax and let the
         sound come from the diaphragm and not from your throat.
             'Pick it up!'
             'No, it's over there!'
             'We need four more!'
             'She's past the last flag, go!'
             'Do you want to drop him in the purple goo?'

EMPHASIS

Some items or words may need to be 'pointed' or stressed and you can do that by highlighting the importance of them in your mind or marking your script and teleprompt. An effective way of alerting the audience to a significant point is to leave a tiny pause just prior to the item or word. When starting a new topic or thought, begin with a fresh approach and on a different note from the one with which you ended your last item. When you come to the end of a topic or thought, finish with energy rather than letting your voice trail off.

PACE

Speed of delivery depends upon the programme subject. Very often nerves can play a great part in determining the rate – either too fast or too slow. Listen to yourself on tape. Try to remain as conversational as possible and remember your desire to communicate. It can help if you keep your intention and thought going right through to the end of the sentence and do not race on too fast into the next subject. Energy and vitality are essential, but stay in control as you still need to be clearly understood.

DICTION AND ARTICULATION

No matter how beautiful the sound is, how varied the pitch or how loud or soft you speak, if your speech is indistinct the viewer won't understand what you're saying.

Spurred on by adrenalin or genuine enthusiasm, some presenters speak so fast that they gabble their words. Alternatively, because they are either tired or are giving a 'relaxed performance', they slur their speech and subsequently become incoherent. Go through your script and search out any words, names or phrases that are difficult to pronounce. Whisper them, exaggerating the pronunciation, and then practise them aloud. Open your mouth, since a tight jaw restricts diction and resonance and it also looks as though you are either frightened or are hiding something! Clarity comes from firm, clear consonants and open vowels. The only way to improve diction and tighten up articulation muscles (the organs of articulation include tongue, teeth, lips, soft palate, hard palate and alveolar ridge) is to exercise and practise. Try tongue-twister exercises to sharpen up your diction.

EXERCISES

(1) Yawn, opening your mouth really wide. Let your jaw drop open. Keep your eyes wide open. Smile very broadly. Then, screw up and tighten every muscle in your face. Repeat the whole exercise. This is to loosen your jaw muscles.

(2) Pucker up your lips and blow kisses. Then smile with your mouth closed.

(3) Imagine that you are chewing a very big sticky sweet and you are trying to dislodge it from your teeth.

(4) Pull your tongue out as far as it will go and flick it up and down and from side to side as fast as you can.

(5) If you have a difficult phrase to speak, grip a pencil between your front teeth and speak the words. Take the pencil out and speak the words again. This exercise forces you to use your organs of articulation and so makes the words clearer.

Sibilance and popping

'S' stands for sibilance. Too much sibilance can sound as if the speaker is hissing, and can be very irritating to the listener. It is also difficult to record such a voice. You can help yourself by de-stressing the 'S' and aiming for the next syllable, or stressing the vowel before the offending 'S'.

'P' stands for 'popping'. Ps and Bs can have an explosive sound if they are over-emphasised. If you are too close to the microphone when you are recording for audio purposes you might be told that you are 'popping' or 'bumping'. Slightly de-stress these consonants or move back a fraction from the microphone. A similar effect can occur with a 'wh' sound, as in 'who'. Over-breathiness can cause a sound like a thud. Use the same remedy of de-stressing or moving back a fraction. Mark your script where you think a danger may occur. In the TV studio popping is not something to worry about, but it is valuable to be aware of it in an audio studio when recording a voice-over (*see* also pp. 129-35).

PRONUNCIATION

There are standard pronunciations for most names and places. If you are in any doubt, look up the word in a dictionary. You can check unusual names with the BBC. When you find the correct pronunciation then write it down clearly – phonetically if you can. Do it so that you can repeat the correct pronunciation the following day or for the next broadcast – e.g. for Mozambique, Moh-zam-beak. It's useful to keep an index for future reference.

Get used to saying the problematic name or word by practising it over and over again. By doing so you will become comfortable with it and sound natural. The dangerous stumbling area is not always the word itself but just before the word as you see it coming up, or just after as you relax at having said it correctly. Practice makes perfect.

FILLERS

Beware of over-using 'extras' – such as 'um', 'er', so', 'well', 'you know'. Natural speech is sprinkled with them, so it's natural to hear them, but try to keep them to a minimum.

IN SUMMARY

Exercises are for development and not to think about in front of the camera. Voice coach Cicely Berry talks about a 'time lag' between recognising the qualities and potential of your voice during exercises and then using your new ability with natural ease. It will take time but will be well worth the effort. Good preparation will enable you to be in control of your whole physical and vocal image.

- Practise reading aloud.
- Warm up your voice with a resonance exercise or a planned warm-up routine.
- Do some simple stretching exercises and keep your torso lifted. Allow breathing space to support your voice. This is good for body language too.
- Stay relaxed and involved.
- Start *on* the first word, not halfway through the sentence.
- Use 'colour' in your intonation, keep words active and alive. Let descriptive words be descriptive.
- Use inflection and vocal range.
- New subject – fresh attack.
- Keep up the pace of delivery but don't gabble.
- Maintain a bright voice: no mumbling or shouting to make your point.
- Keep your energy running through to the end of the sentence. Try not to drop off the volume as you come to the finish.
- Over-pronounce words rather than murmuring and slurring. Articulate and be understood.
- In hard news reporting or factual corporate presentation, don't over-emphasise or stress words too heavily. Use your lower range with authority.

5

Fighting Fears

First and foremost, it's natural to be nervous before a performance of any kind. I know of no really good presenters who fail to feel an edge of anticipation before they start work. Nerves concentrate the mind and force you to focus on the job in hand. As presenter Siân Lloyd puts it, 'Nerves give you a tingle of anticipation . . . it's important to be yourself.'

Without nerves there is a tendency to become complacent, which may be interpreted by the viewer as arrogance. Preparation may become a little less precise, which in turn leads to mistakes creeping in. So a few butterflies can be good for you. It's when nerves get the upper hand, preventing you from giving your best, that you need to act and take control.

WHAT CAN YOU DO IF YOU GET A FIT OF NERVES?

One early step is to identify what it is that is making you nervous. Is it:

- fear of forgetting what you are saying or doing
- fear of making a fool of yourself
- fear of not being good enough
- fear of not being liked?

Once you have done this, you can then begin to address your reaction to the fear, and take positive action to combat it. You can even use the built-up nervous energy to your advantage, giving your whole presentation enhanced spirit and vigour. First of all, identify the cause of your nervousness, then acknowledge your reaction – i.e. how it manifests itself. Then, use the power of that energy in a positive way.

As discussed in Chapter 2, if you have created a persona that is not true to you, it may fall apart when tensions increase. Remember, 'Arrogance is the mask that fear wears. You have no need to be frightened of yourself.' So be yourself.

Nerves can take many forms, both physical and psychological, and have a nasty knack of sneaking up on you. They can result in hot, sticky, trembling hands; shaking legs; a clenching stomach; a dry mouth; a thumping heart; feelings of hot or cold; nausea; and frequent trips to the loo! Tension in the neck and shoulders can impair your speech, producing a constricted, pinched sound or a quivering voice, and in extreme cases it can lead to a loss of voice or even permanent damage. Some people show their nervousness by getting very bossy or demanding, or displaying unexpected emotional outbursts. So – what is happening?

Our bodies have an automatic defence mechanism that is engineered to react to danger. This is an instinctive reaction. The autonomic nervous system does not recognise the nature of the danger, only that there is a perceived threat. Fear, which is what nerves are, has aided our survival; when our ancestors were confronted by a sabre-toothed tiger, they were filled with fear and either fought for their lives or fled – fight or flight. When you are presenting you are not under any physical threat, but that's not to say that your fears are not real. The sense of not being in control is the same, and our autonomic nervous system reacts in the same way as it has done for thousands of years, unaware that running screaming from the building or lashing out violently at the camera (the object of fear) or anyone nearby is not the most appropriate way of dealing with the situation!

In such situations a whole range of glands and hormones in your body are activated, the ones having the most obvious effect being the adrenal glands. These release cortisol, noradrenalin and adrenalin into the bloodstream, effectively preparing the body for any alarming eventuality. In order to be in this high state of alert, essential organs such as the heart, lungs and major muscles take priority in the demand for much-needed oxygenated blood. The heart beats faster, pumping this blood to where it is most required. Muscles flex and tighten. More oxygen is needed and so breathing becomes shallow and rapid; stored glycogen is rapidly converted into glucose, a primary source of energy. The body's physical appearance changes slightly too, showing any potential attacker that this animal (you) is ready for a fight and is not to be messed with. Sweating palms give a better grip, pupils dilate to give better vision, and hair stands up on end to improve physical awareness as well as to make us look scary! Every change we feel when we are nervous is by way of preparation for 'fight or flight'. But is looking and feeling like a cornered cat any way to face a camera and present a TV programme?

What do you do, then, with this build-up of energy? If you do nothing, levels of blood sugar and adrenalin remain unnecessarily high for longer than we might wish and stay 'on standby for action'. This is where a series of short, sharp muscle exercises and slow breathing exercises can help to use up that excess energy, slow your heart rate and release some tension. Learning to relax is one of the most valuable skills you can acquire as a presenter. And, yes, it is a skill and does need practice. Initially, it may seem impossible to switch into a relaxed state in a matter of seconds, but once you have found your own particular trigger it should become easy.

There are plenty of books on fighting fears and nerve control, and there are calming tapes or CDs that can help you. Listed below are some useful exercises and strategies – but always remember that all the exercises in the world won't replace thorough preparation and rehearsal.

EXERCISES TO HELP YOU REGAIN CONTROL

Relaxation

Try to set some time aside each day for relaxation. It need only be 5–10 minutes, but it helps if you can make it a regular routine. A few minutes' relaxation is like a holiday, a brief respite from all the anxiety that's building up, helping you to return to work with new energy and keener concentration. As well as preparing you physically, relaxation takes your mind away from those nerves – the butterflies, the dry mouth and the trembling.

Choose a form of exercise that works best for you when you are on your own. Also, find another exercise you *can* do in public, for those moments when a rush of panic or tension attacks. You need to be able to do your exercises not only in your dressing room, but in the loo or behind the set, and actually on set too.

EXERCISES

Start these exercises in a quiet spot at home. The more you practise them, the easier they will be to refer to when you need them. Turn the phone off. This is your time – value it.

(1) Sit comfortably or lie down with a small cushion under your head. Breathe gently and easily; close your eyes if you want to.

(2) In the same position breathe in through your nose for a slow count of 5 and out through your mouth for a slow count of 5. Do this 5 times. With each exhalation relax your body into the floor.

(3) Remain where you are, and starting at your feet, let your mind do a 'body sweep' – consciously relaxing each area of your body until you reach the top of your head.

(4) Once you have done the 'body sweep', you can begin focusing more specifically on each muscle group. Again,

start with your feet and then work through the body.
Breathe in as you tense each muscle group and breathe out
as you relax.

Breathing and stretching

Select the exercises which work best for you and create your own,
personalised relaxation regime. If you know any yoga or Alexander
Technique exercises, they may well prove useful too.

EXERCISES

(1) Standing with an easy, straight posture and your feet slightly
apart, wrap your arms around your body.
Breathe in and hug and squeeze yourself tightly. You will
find that your spine naturally curves around, so tuck your
head into your chest as it does so.
Breathe out. Release your arms and step out to the side,
head up, arms relaxed by your side. Breathe in gently and
stand up straight. Breathe out.
Shake out any tension from your arms and hands. Repeat 2
or 3 times.

(2) Breathe in and lift your arms forwards and up above your head.
Stretch up and feel your ribs 'lifting out' of your hips.
Stretch your fingers and, as you breathe in, release your
arms out to the sides and bring them slowly down. Repeat.

(3) Breathe in and as you do, raise your arms up at the side and
stretch them up above your head. Breathe out as you release
them forwards and down to a count of 10.

(4) Drop your head forwards and then lift it up again.
Now, keeping your head facing front, drop your right ear
towards your right shoulder and bring it back to the centre
again.
Do the same towards the left. Repeat.

(5) Shrug your shoulders up and down.
Lift them up to your ears, then roll them to the back,
squeezing the shoulder blades together.
Press the shoulders down and roll them round to the front,
then up to your ears and finally drop them down.
Shrug them up and down.
Repeat the circle until you feel that your shoulders are
relaxed.

(6) Clench your fists tightly and then flex your fingers. Repeat
several times. Shake out any tension.

(7) Clench your feet tightly and then flex them. Repeat several times. Circle each foot a few times in each direction.

ATTITUDE

'If I get nervous before a really important event, I relax and remember that it's just TV, not life or death. Just relax.'
Jon Snow (Channel 4 News)

Understanding the physical cause of nerves is part of the strategy to combat them. Understanding what it is you are fundamentally frightened of is another part. Now it's time to change your mental attitude. If, when you feel the rush of adrenalin, you become victim to the sensation, you're on a slippery slope. Here, then, are some alternative suggestions:

- Remember that you are not going to be eaten by a woolly backed stregathaurus. No one is going to die.
- Acknowledge that your body is gearing up for you to perform to the best of your ability, and not preparing you to fight or flee the building. All the physical reactions are making you more aware, alert and keeping you on your toes.
- As your body pumps with adrenalin, regard the sensations as a rush of excitement – not fear.
- Close your eyes. Visualise yourself in a calm, quiet place. Breathe. Open your eyes.
- When you choose your 'friend' in the camera lens really identify them and talk to them.
- Focus on the task ahead, regarding this as an opportunity to share information or to entertain. Put yourself second to the information that you're imparting, or to the viewers' overall enjoyment of the show. In other words, stop thinking about yourself.
- Visualise the point of victory – the end of a successful show, with everyone congratulating each other – and sense your own satisfaction.

If time is short or if you get a rush of nerves in front of the camera, first and foremost remember to breathe slowly and deeply.

Many people find the following effective in helping them to relax and fight nerves.

- Acupuncture
- Aromatherapy
- Alexander Technique
- Autogenic training
- Flower remedies
- Homeopathy
- Hypnotherapy
- Massage

- Meditation
- Naturopathy
- Osteopathy
- Reiki
- Reflexology
- Shiatsu
- T'ai Chi
- Yoga

It really doesn't matter how you get rid of your nerves – or if people on the set think that you're a little crazy when you practise your relaxation technique. What matters is that you get rid of tension and fear.

WHAT THEY SAY

'Nerves aren't a bad thing. Once you get your first couple of lines out you start enjoying it. I always talk to people, and when it comes to the camera, it's just one of them I'm talking to. Meeting stars, maybe I get nervous for one in ten. I was nervous before meeting Whitney Houston, but that's understandable!'
Trevor Nelson (MTV, BBC Radio 1)

'My first day on SKY TV, I had no training and I went on live. I was so scared I wanted to be sick. My face wouldn't work properly: one side of my mouth seemed to lock. If someone had said, "You can go home now," I'd have run. But I knew after that day I would never, ever have to be that nervous again. And I haven't been.'
Suzi Perry (SKY Sports and BBC City Hospital)

'I've been very nervous but it's never stopped me doing what I wanted to do. I breathe deeply and I sing. I say, "I love doing this." At beauty contests I used to walk around nightclubs in a swimsuit. How ridiculous is that? I was very nervous but I used to sing or listen to the music and enjoy each song as I walked along. Now I sing the songs in my head. Motivational songs like M People or "You'll never walk alone".'
Debbie Greenwood (BBC Breakfast Time, UK Living)

'Whilst presenting a live television show, I forgot some words and there was no autocue. I said, "I am terribly sorry, I have forgotten your name."
Cheryl Baker (How Dare You, Record Breakers)

'It's crucial not to be nervous. It's easy to communicate unease to a viewer without realising it and they immediately pick up on it.'
Jeremy Vine (BBC Newsnight)

'Walking towards camera on location, inevitably my wires got caught under a stepping stone which was at the side of a foot-bridge. My leg got stuck. I couldn't move, and I had to get over to my mark. I just had to say "hang on a minute", untangle my leg, gather the lead up under my arm and carry on. After any disastrous presenting situation you have to learn you can get yourself out of a hole and that you won't go to pieces. You are no longer nervous, so therefore you have no fear of it. It's familiarity.'
Jeff Moody (Channel 5 Weather)

'My first piece to camera, I looked like a startled rabbit! I shook all the way through it. I had no preparation. I had a glass of water which I was unable to pick up because I was shaking so much. I got over it through practice.'
Sophie Raworth (BBC Breakfast News)

6

Preparing for the Studio

The day has arrived for you to go to the TV studio. It may be for a screen test, as a guest presenter, as an interviewee, or the first day of many working days. Whatever the occasion, your preparation should be the same. (For a screen test, refer also to pp. 170-3).

Leave enough time to get to the studio early. There's nothing worse than arriving there feeling hot and sticky and in a panic, worried that you don't have enough time to do all that you're supposed to. If you're arriving by car, take a walk around the building and get some air. Take time to clear your head – you may have been stuck in traffic, driven at speed down the motorway, or travelled by public transport. Stand up straight, stretch out, breathe, and focus your attention on the task in hand. From now on you need to have all your wits about you.

Remember that first impressions are all-important; from the moment you enter the studio premises the spotlight is on you. If this is your first visit to the studio, make sure that you have all the relevant contact names and telephone numbers close at hand. Report to reception – you will either be collected or directed to where you need to be. Make sure all the relevant people know that you have arrived and know where you will be if needed. This is the time when people will introduce themselves to you; try to remember their names and any important information they give you.

If you have a dressing room, use this as a place to relax and prepare. Organise your clothes, check that they are as you want them. You may wish to hang your jacket up to prevent it from getting creased. If you haven't been given a dressing room it's likely that you will be shown somewhere out of the way of technical preparations that you can use as your private refuge. In all the hustle and bustle of the studio it's important to find yourself an area, no matter how small, which you can call your own. Be prepared for time schedules to change. One moment you think you have tons of time and you seem to be sitting around doing very little; the next moment you are racing through a piece of script or being hurried into camera shot. The more you can prepare yourself in the quiet moments, the more in control you will be when the pressure is on.

SOME NECESSARY TASKS

There are a few tasks which need to be completed, the order of which invariably alters. These include: liaising with the producer and director, acknowledging guests, checking and re-editing scripts, make-up, wardrobe and personal preparation.

The script
If the producer or director hasn't found you, then find them. There may be a read-through of the script, but if not, you need to know if there are any changes. If so what, and what else does that affect?

- Confirm the running order and make alterations where necessary.
- Confirm (and view if necessary) any recorded inserts – VTs.
- Clearly number script pages and cue cards.
- Does your script tally with the teleprompter? This can either wait until you get into the studio, or you may want to give it to the PA to pass on to the teleprompt operator. If it's self-driven, then do it yourself.
- Are there any names that are difficult to pronounce? Note them and practise if there's time.
- Check your 'intros' and 'outros' (*see* also pp. 83-93).
- Check that all current information is relevant and up-to-date.
- If you have any new items to include, then rehearse them. Keep them short and upbeat.

Guests
Take the time to introduce yourself to them. It is polite and puts them at ease; you will also have a slightly clearer idea of who you are inter-viewing. In addition, they may give you some new or more recent information. However, don't be tempted to stay chatting with them. Do the pleasantries, get the information you need and go. You may only need to say 'hello'.

Personal props
Check that you have a working pen and earpiece, and that your cue cards are in the correct order. Collect and check any prop that you will need in the studio. If you are doing your own make-up (men and women), take a powder compact with you into the studio to make sure your forehead, nose and chin don't glisten and shine. You might even like to take in a brush or comb (*see* also p. 190, *A Presenter's Survival Kit*).

Make-up

Allow enough time. If there's a make-up artist provided, check what time you are expected. Their schedule often changes and so be prepared either to wait a little bit longer or be seen straightaway: try to be flexible. You'll find that being in make-up gives you a few precious moments to relax. If you are doing your own, check that you have everything that you need and give yourself time to apply it. If the producer, assistant director or floor manager finds you during make-up, be prepared to be a sitting duck for whatever information they have to throw at you. Take your script and a pen with you to jot down any notes.

Physical preparation

Give yourself time to practise any form of relaxation or any vocal exercises which you find useful. The following are some useful guidelines for physical preparation.

- Try not to drink too much caffeine. You'll have enough adrenalin rushing around your body to keep you alert when you hit the studio: an excess can make you hyperactive.
- Limit the amount of milky products you drink directly before you speak, as they have a tendency to clog up the vocal passage. Unfortunately, chocolate has the same effect.
- Avoid carbonated water and drinks as they can make you burp.
- Eat sparingly, but do eat something. It could be a long session.
- Absolutely no alcohol! Even a small glass can dull the senses and give a false sense of confidence, the results not being what you would like to remember after the programme is over. It could also cost you your job. You can treat yourself to a drink afterwards. No chemical stimulants or relaxants either.
- Shake out physical tension by doing some gentle stretches.
- Free up shoulders and neck, jaw, and organs of articulation.
- Hum to gently warm up your voice.
- Breathe to relax and to control yourself.
- Check your clothing, shoelaces, hair, loose jewellery and watches.
- Remove loose change and keys from your pockets. Turn off or silence pagers, telephones, digital watches and personal organisers.
- Go to the toilet! Then re-check your clothing.
- When you are called, or when studio time is approaching, don't hesitate but go there directly.

Part Two

IN THE STUDIO

7

Who's Who and What's What

You should know the names of the producer and director, the PA and the floor manager. It shows professionalism and helps to create a good working atmosphere. It's worthwhile writing their names down on your script or running order so that you will remember them. Also refer to Insiders Jargon, pp.183-9.

GENERAL JOB DESCRIPTIONS

These are listed below in no particular order:

Producer (Prod.) And/or executive producer. Will usually have been with the show since its inception, or at least since its early days.
The employer who brings together the members of the production team, including a casting director if applicable.
Responsible for the financial aspects of the show as well as its format and content.
In the studio keeps a close eye on the script, authorises and often instigates script changes.

Director (Dir.) Responsible for the visual presentation of the show.
Co-ordinates with lighting, sound, design and cameras to get the best picture.
Calls the camera shots.
Will talk to the presenter (sometimes directly on talkback, sometimes via the floor manager), giving instructions in order to achieve the best visual appearance.

Production Assistant (PA) Types up scripts.
Works out the crew, presenter and cast calls.
Ensures programme timings are adhered to, liaising with the floor manager and cueing the presenter via talkback.
Assists the producer and director in all communications (meetings, phone calls, filling in necessary forms and general correspondence).

Editor Liaises with the producer and sometimes the presenter regarding script content, wording and phrasing.

Tape Editor Post-production editing of the programme.

Vision Mixer (VM) On the director's cue, cuts to each camera shot as scripted or on ad lib cue.

Camera Operator Operates the camera focus and moves under the director's instruction.

Technical Co-ordinator Ensures that all lines of communication are operable and facilities available. Liaises with all technical staff and sources. Responsible for any technical requirements.

Make-up and Wardrobe Ultimately responsible to the producer but should always be sensitive to the presenter's needs!

Designer Works with the producer and director on the show's visual style.

Sound Engineer/Supervisor (SS) Checks and maintains balance of show's sound output as well as monitoring levels for the talkback.

Lighting Engineer/Supervisor (LS) Lights the studio in accordance with the wishes of the producer and the designer.

Visual Effects Designer/Supervisor Designs or works with the designer and crew to operate any special effect, e.g. smoke, rain, collapsing furniture or scenery.

Teleprompt Operator (autocue; autoscript) Controls the speed of script you see rolling up in front of the camera lens (*see* also Chapter 10, *The Teleprompt*).

Fireman A safety officer is legally required to be in the studio during recording.

Floor Manager (FM) Can, and should be, your very best friend! A person of many parts who liaises with the director, all technical and production staff, and on-the-screen performers. In some cases a floor manager works as an assistant director. Main responsibility is to ensure a smooth-running show from the studio.

Is in constant contact with the gallery and able to guide studio floor crew through the show, cueing effects, cue and title cards and scenic and action moves.

Counts aloud or signals start and/or finish of show (or VT OB link-up where applicable). Cues the action with precision, ensuring a clean start and finish to each item or scene or move.

Checks all props, scenery and furniture, and checks the studio for obstructions, fire and safety hazards.

Ensures punctuality, observation of scheduled times and studio breaks. Confirms that all studio access doors are shut, that monitors are working and that *everyone* is standing by ready for action.

(*Note*: Whilst on call, filming in the studio or on location, *always* tell the floor manager or assistant director if you are leaving the studio or set, explaining why and when you are coming back. At the end of recording or transmission, *always* check with the floor manager or assistant director for clearance and check your next call time.)

THE DIRECTOR AND THE PRESENTER

With a nod and a wink to Rogers and Hammerstein and *Oklahoma!*, the director and presenter should be friends! There does need to be a common understanding and tolerance between them, and certainly, both need an awareness of each other's jobs and the pressure and demands involved. Both need to exercise boundless patience with each other under the most trying of circumstances. The reality is that whilst the presenter must convey calm and control, very often the director displays anything but! Try not to pick up any tension or negative influences: this requires discipline and a cool head, and you must filter only what is applicable to you. Don't become involved in any technical issues, and don't start taking over direction from the studio floor. Keep to your own job, however, helpful you intend to be. If you do have a suggestion, give it to the floor manager to pass on. You can further help the director by listening at all times. If you don't have an earpiece or talkback, then pay attention to what's going on around you and listen to the floor manager.

You will need to train yourself to keep an ear open for new directions, listening to commands at the same time as speaking to the viewers. You need to be kept up to date with new information – especially in a live programme – and directors don't expect to have to repeat themselves.

Respond immediately, otherwise you will have the director screaming in your ear. Any preparation you can do in advance of the programme is a help: it will make you feel better, and give the director confidence in you. It's essential that your line of communication – whether that's via an earpiece or the floor manager – is clear from the outset. (There are plenty of pre-programme checks you can make; these are covered later in the book.) Always keep to the script. If the programme encourages loose chat it is still important to keep to the agreed cue for key items.

Ideally, any presenter would like to be given confidence and reassurance throughout the programme, but because of the many demands on the director it's very rare. So don't get paranoid if no one says that you are fantastic. Everyone has a job to do and is usually fantastic at it. Try handing out a few compliments yourself at the end of the day. You may be nicely rewarded.

A SELECTION OF FREQUENTLY ASKED STUDIO QUESTIONS

(Q) When can I talk to the director from the studio floor?
(A) When you're not live on air. Be sensitive to what's going on in the production gallery, and choose the most opportune moment.

(Q) Can I move the chairs or furniture?
(A) Not unless you've cleared it with the floor manager first. They are likely to have been put on 'marks' to gain the best lighting effect or camera shot. Chairs off the set are equally important, even if nobody seems to be using them. They may have been set there to be used later on in the programme. In short, *don't move anything.*

(Q) Can I get up and walk about?
(A) Once you are on set, always check with the floor manager before leaving your position. The director may be lining up shots and need you to stay where you are. You are almost as important during rehearsal as in transmission.

Never cross in front of the cameras; the director may be setting up another shot or the operator may be focusing the shot. If you need to reposition to another part of the set, *don't* walk in front of the camera unless specifically directed to as part of the action. Get used to walking behind the camera at all times.

(Q) Can I smoke?
(A) Not in the studio unless you are directed to do so.

(Q) Where can I leave my valuables and dressing room key?
(A) You don't always get a dressing room and if you do it may not have a safe. Don't bring unnecessary valuables – i.e. money and precious jewels – with you. Give your key to your dresser or ask the floor manager where you may leave it or any valuable belongings.

(Q) Can I take my coffee or tea into the studio?
(A) No, not unless you are directed to do so. If you really need a drink, ask the floor manager. Don't expect to keep it though – the floor manager will need to make sure it's out of vision, safely away from electrics.

(Q) Can I bring in friends and family?
(A) No. This is a workplace. If you have a live audience, that's different: they can sit with the audience. But in general it's not advisable to have people wandering about. Primarily, it's a safety issue and you won't be able to look after them as you have a job to concentrate on. There may be an occasion when the director will let someone 'sit in' the gallery, but it'll be a favour, so ask nicely.

COMMON CAMERA SHOTS AND INSTRUCTIONS

Some of these sound like coded messages – and in fact, that's what they are. It's all in the name of efficiency and it usually works. However, as a presenter you should know what they all mean, especially as they affect you and your image on screen.

So, preparing or cueing to take the picture for broadcast from a nominated camera, you may hear the following.
COMING TO CAMERA 2

Taking the picture for broadcast from a nominated camera – TAKE 2 or ON 2.

Camera moves

REPO
A command to the camera operator to reposition to a different location or pre-agreed angle on the set. Camera command will be – REPO CAM 1 TO . . .

PAN
Camera turns from right to left. The camera command is – PAN LEFT.
Camera turns from left to right. The camera command is – PAN RIGHT.
Camera focuses from low to high. The camera command is – PAN UP.
Camera focuses from high to low. The camera command is – PAN
DOWN.

TILT
Camera points upwards or downwards.
The camera command is – TILT UP or TILT DOWN.

ELEVATE and DEPRESS
Raising and lowering the camera on its column.
The camera command is – ELEVATE or DEPRESS.

CRAB
The camera moves sideways to right or left.
The camera command is – CRAB LEFT or CRAB RIGHT.

TRACKING
Moving the camera directly towards or away from the subject.
It more clearly resembles what is seen by the human eye, as the body
moves towards the subject – unlike the zoom (*see* below) which magni-
fies the subject.
The camera command is – TRACK IN or TRACK OUT.

ZOOM
In fact, this is not a camera movement but a change of vision, using
the camera lens to magnify the subject for a more detailed view. The
shot is usually focused on a stationary subject.
The camera command is – ZOOM IN or ZOOM OUT.

CLOSE-UP
Sometimes the director will use a combination of *tracking* and *zooming*.
The camera commands will be – GO IN FOR A CLOSE-UP. TIGHTEN;
LOOSEN. GO IN; COME OUT.

Camera shots
Different directors have slightly different ideas of how these terms of
framing actually appear. So the photographs below are a generalised
interpretation of each shot.

Long shot

Medium long shot

Mid shot

Medium close up

Close up

8

Preparing for Action

A studio is any space in which you can record or transmit. It may vary in size from a vast barn of a building to a small garage or converted bedroom. The larger space will have huge scene dock doors to allow movement of sets and a floor space big enough to drive cars into. There may even be room to seat an audience of a few hundred people. Lighting will be rigged from a ceiling 30 ft high. There will be cameras and sound equipment, and large cables snaking their way across the floor. Most studios are soundproofed to keep out extraneous noise and all should have fire doors. The filming area is divided into areas to help both camera and director to frame locations.

Whatever the size of the studio, the basic principles of presentation apply: the camera is still focusing on you, and you are talking to the one person in the camera lens.

IN A FULLY CREWED STUDIO

First, introduce yourself to everyone. If it's appropriate, make a brief visit to the gallery. Your contact in the studio is the floor manager; refer to them at all times. Ask them if it's alright to test out whatever you are going to sit on, lean on, walk over, step on, hang from or pull down! Wait until you are given the go-ahead, as the piece of set or scenery may not have been bolted down as yet – and then try out the move. Familiarise yourself with the studio layout, allowing plenty of time to organise yourself and feel at ease. Try out your chair, if you have one. Sit on the edge of the desk, walk up and down stairs and rostra. Don't move anything unless you've been asked to. Make yourself as comfortable as possible and eliminate any potential surprises.

Put your script, notes or cue cards where you want them and tell the floor manager where they are so that they won't be moved without your knowledge. If you have any props, ensure that they are within easy reach or make arrangements for them to be handed to you. Liaise with the prompt operator (*see* also pp. 76-83). It's very likely that the director will want to rehearse the opening shots: this is a useful rehearsal for you too.

SKY TV gallery

Studio layout

Be obliging at all times and remind yourself that a good show relies on teamwork. This might be a good time to check with the director that the running order has not been changed and that all VT inserts are as you've agreed. It's vital that the communication line to the gallery is clear so check that your talkback is working. At this point your sensitivity and patience will be most valued by everyone around you. Do not shout demands but wait until you can reasonably attract attention. Talk to the floor manager and ask them to pass on your requests. Clarify which camera you will be addressing at any one time, and if you are in any doubt, check and make a note of it on your script.

Once you've been fitted with a microphone, don't interfere with it. The sound department will be striving to get the best sound quality: if you move the mic after you've been tested for sound and balanced, you will change the sound quality – but the engineer won't know that until you speak out again and that may not be until the programme has begun. If you have a problem, tell the floor manager, who will contact sound.

The output TV monitor needs to be where you can see it, but not in your direct line of sight (or you may end up watching yourself). Don't try to move the monitor yourself, check with the floor manager. When everything is in place, take a few deep breaths. Check your appearance, your clothes, hair and make-up, and – maintaining an unruffled demeanour – stay alert and aware of everything around you.

WHEN YOU'RE ON YOUR OWN

Currently, this applies mainly to link presenters and news readers. However, it's a fast-changing world, so it's possible that more and more presenters may soon find themselves on their own. In order to cut down on personnel, the presenter is expected to become a 'one-man band'. Without a floor manager you are dependent on talkback and will need to be very skilled in its use. You are not alone in experiencing staff reduction: directors, for example, very often have to combine their skills with vision-mixing. Multi-skilling is becoming more and more common. Ralph Jones of LWT's *The Lab* works with teams of two or three producer/director/presenters who are skilled in camera and lighting operation. He says that this breaks down the old-style hierarchy and to a certain extent frees up the presenter: 'They could be given a camera and just go, effectively blurring the line between documentary subject and presenter. If an up-and-coming presenter has an idea of their own, and the nous to do it, they can set up their own programme. Technology isn't a stumbling block.'

You will never be sent into a studio on your own without training and familiarisation. Your preparation before entering the studio will be much the same, but you will need to double-check that you have everything you need as there is no one to run for you. (This is when the Presenter's Survival Kit comes into its own – *see* p. 190.) Take a glass or bottle of water into the studio with you, in case your throat gets dry, but place it at a distance away from you and the computer to avoid nasty accidents.

When you arrive, make a brief visit to the gallery if you have the time. Alternatively, acknowledge everyone from the studio floor. Although you are alone in the studio you can be reassured that the director will be in constant contact with you from the production gallery. The first thing you need to do is get into position in camera vision so that everyone in the gallery will know that you're there. Programme the computer and prompt to show your script but, before you study it, attend to the necessary technical details. An engineer will set up a general lighting state, which can be marginally altered from the gallery. A camera will be locked off, in position and with a general focus. A duty engineer may come and re-focus but won't necessarily operate. Make sure that the camera is where you want it to be and that you can see the prompt screen clearly. If it needs moving, tell the gallery and hopefully someone will come to your assistance. If no one is there to help you – and in this instance, it will be very rare – you may have to do it yourself. Only do it if you are absolutely sure you know what you are doing; cameras are heavy, but delicate and extremely expensive, and it is preferable to wait for a technician. The output TV monitor should be at the edge of your line of sight and be programmed to relay *your* programme and not online to another studio! You should be able to change channel from the studio floor.

Sound is checked in the gallery but you are responsible for fitting your own microphone. Make sure the power switch on the mic pack is 'on', then fasten the mic pack on to your waist belt or put it into your pocket. Thread the wire up the front of your jacket or dress and clip the mic on to a lapel or neckline. A good position is in the centre of your chest just above the heart line. When you initially receive your mic pack from the sound department, check with them whether they prefer the microphone itself to be pointing up towards your chin or down towards your waist.

Whether sitting or standing, settle yourself into a comfortable position. Connect your earpiece to the talkback and ask the production gallery if they can hear you. They may not respond immediately but as long as you remain in camera vision they will communicate with you as soon as they can. Confirm that the running order is as you expect and note any changes. Put your script, notes or cue cards where you can easily reach them. If you have any props, be confident that they are also within easy reach. When you are on your own, it's more than likely that you'll be working a self-operated prompt so be sure that the whole system is running smoothly. Roll through your script, confirming any changes. Find a comfortable reading speed and rehearse your opening lines. Practise intros and outros of any difficult links with the prompt.

Finally, check your appearance – adjust your clothes, hair and make-up.

> 'Just me in a studio with a locked-off camera. Quite bizarre – quite intimate.'
> *Kate MacIntyre (Channel 5)*

One minute to TX

Keep calm, breathe and focus. This is a moment of neutral time. Gather your thoughts and energies ready to respond when the cue is given.

- Remind yourself of your opening movement and lines.
- Ensure that the prompt text is lined up where you want it to begin.
- Sit or stand in readiness, with energy in your posture.
- Breathe in deeply. Keep your shoulders down.
- Slowly exhale three-quarters of the breath.
- Shake out any tension.
- Smile to release tight facial muscles.

5 seconds to TX

- Breathe in, but not too deeply.
- As you breathe out and on cue, focus directly into the camera lens.

Over to you . . .

9

Cueing

Everyone in the studio works to cues. Cues are a signal for action or for speech. In order to keep the programme running smoothly, all the departments – camera, sound, lighting, VT (videotape operator), vision mixer – have to respond at their given time, or 'on cue'.

The vocabulary used in making a feature film and TV drama differs slightly from that used in current affairs and light entertainment programming. A simple example is the direction to start. For film drama, and even some commercials where the director is used to film work, you will hear, 'and . . . action' as the cue. The TV presenter will hear 'and . . . cue'. The response to the direction, however it is received, must be immediate and, whenever possible, anticipated. There are also different methods of cueing, the most common being 'talkback' which you receive through an earpiece. If you are not using this method – and in corporate presentation it's used infrequently – then pay keen attention to the floor manager or stage manager. (In corporate work the action is frequently controlled by a 'show caller' who may well have to take on the responsibilities of a producer and floor manager. Make sure you can see their signals clearly and that you understand *exactly* what they mean.)

The trick for the TV presenter is to register which is *your* cue amongst all the other cues which are being given. For instance, if you are using an earpiece you may hear, 'camera 1, cue' or 'cue VT', 'roll VT', or 'cue Joanne'. Directors often try to build the presenter's reaction time into the cueing sequence (i.e. the time between the cue being given and the presenter actually getting out the first word). For example, the count coming out of a VT insert could be, '5, 4, 3, 2, cue Joanne and cut'. In this way, the presenter's voice will come in hard at the end of the VT, far slicker than having a slight pause before the presenter speaks. Confirm before transmission how you will be cued and listen carefully for your own cue. A late response or an early start can look clumsy and inefficient. Worse still, you may get half your sentence chopped off as another segment of the programme is timed and cued to begin. Technically, this is called 'crashing'. Or you may start before the camera has cut to you and then be left looking blankly at the camera because you finished too early. If you are late responding to your cue for an action you will be 'out of synch' with everyone else. It's possible that a camera shot may miss you altogether, as you were late to walk into the picture; or you could get hurt if the cue was to duck an incoming missile!

For cueing to work well, there must be a great element of trust. For instance, if the floor manager cues you to start but the light on the camera which you've been directed to address isn't on – go anyway. It may be a cross fade, or perhaps another camera is picking you up at the director's choice. If you've been cued don't wait or look for the camera which *you* think is appropriate. You've been cued: get on with it.

Most VTs begin on an instant start (or an instant roll). That is, they play almost immediately after a cue is given. At one time a run-in of 5 seconds was required to get a tape up to speed. That is now only common in filming, but you will be counted out of a videotape item. It means being counted back from the VT insert to the presenter in the studio. You will hear from the PA, 'Coming back to the studio in 10, . . . in 5, 4, 3, 2, 1 and cue.' It's usual to get a vocal or signed 10-second count into and out of an interview, a live insert, a commercial break or any key item. These are the count cues you need to listen and look out for to ensure clean and smooth links.

Don't feel tempted to change the text of your script without first checking with the director, especially where it leads into a VT or a key item in the running order of the programme. The rest of the studio team may well be waiting for your word or phrase cue, and if it is not given as it is written down in the script they will be confused and the result could be a messy link. Not good news if you are the one in vision.

Methods of cueing a presenter vary. Here are some of the most common.

METHODS OF CUEING

Talkback

Vital instructions can be given to you directly by the producer, director or PA in the production gallery via a talkback earpiece. This is an essential piece of equipment for the TV presenter and working with talkback is an essential skill. The earpiece is a piece of clear plastic that should be moulded to fit unobtrusively into your ear. It works just like a hearing aid. In fact, any hearing-aid shop can provide you with one, once they have taken a mould of your ear shape. You will then have your own custom-made, snugly fitting, comfortable earpiece. It is attached by a clear plastic tube to the talkback equipment – so that the director, literally, has your ear! – and works as a loudspeaker, resonating sound along the tube so that you can hear what is being said. Some have a small hole to allow in ambient noise.

The latest versions are wireless and are widely used in large TV studios where the presenter moves around a lot, as well as by singers for 'foldback' (a singer may want to hear selected voices or instruments with which to blend their own voice)

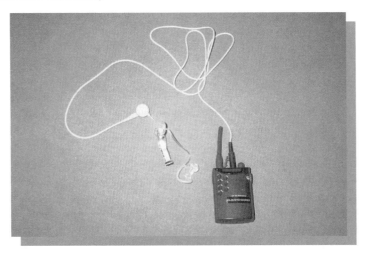

Talkback pack and earpiece

'Originally, I found talkback terrifying. I found myself repeating numbers, counting along with the PA's count and answering back to the gallery. Three voices constantly giving me three sets of information from the gallery, plus writing something for the next interview plus reading the wires for eight hours on air. You'd be so stricken with fear if you couldn't take it in.'
Lisa Aziz (Sky News)

'Talkback used to freak me out, but now I find it comforting. I don't think it helps to panic.'
Kate MacIntyre (Channel 5 Youth Programmes)

Open talkback
This is when you can hear everything that is being said in the gallery. You have to be very disciplined to listen only to what is being directed at you, and to filter out everything else. You also need to be able to maintain a conversation with your guest, or continue talking to the viewers, whilst listening and responding to the producer or director who is giving you instructions in your ear – and without any visible signs of distraction. Occasionally, if it is not important for you to hear everything, the director

will turn off open talkback, in which case the talkback will only be turned back on when necessary, leaving you to get on with the show. This is called 'switch talkback' or 'keyed talkback'. The volume is regulated by the sound engineer in the gallery and you should arrange to set a level with them before the show.

Lazy talkback

This is used mainly on live programmes, and consists of a direct line from the presenter's mic fed to a separate talkback speaker in the gallery. In this way a two-way conversation can happen during a commercial break or VT inserts.

Whatever you do, don't 'talk back' to the talkback during the programme itself! Also resist the temptation to put your hand up to the earpiece – the whole idea of talkback is that you can seamlessly continue presenting whilst receiving important information and updates. If the earpiece fits well there should be no need to adjust its placing, but if however it does come adrift whilst you are 'on air', then try to replace it when the camera is not on you or during a VT insert. Alternatively let the viewer know you have a slight problem and ask them to bear with you whilst you put it right.

The studio TV monitor

It's often possible to take a visual cue from a specific action on the VT or from a live insert. You can do this by watching the monitor that is showing the transmission output. Often, some live action may be happening in another part of the studio and you can't see it from where you are. The floor manager should be there to cue you, and you may have talkback, but having a monitor nearby keeps you in touch with what the viewer is seeing.

Try to find out what your visual cue is. The director or PA will know what the last shot or action is and will be able to help you. You can also ask the director, 'What is the "out" on this item?' (meaning, what is your cue to start). You may have the opportunity to view a pre-recorded VT before the programme. If you can watch it, it will help with your pick-up and link into the next item; you don't want to get caught out by a sudden and abrupt finish, so eliminate the surprises.

Having a visual cue gives you a few valuable seconds to prepare and it puts you in control. For a very natural feel, presenters often look up from the monitor (which may or may not be in shot) just after having received their cue. It's useful if you are referring to the last report in the link, for example: 'That film was shot two hours before the earthquake.' Some directors like to know beforehand that this is your style so that they don't panic, thinking that you haven't heard their cue.

Word cues

You can take a cue from a word or phrase from the previous item. Check with the director that the script is the same as the one you have, and that nothing has been edited out. Whether you have a script or not, try to watch any pre-recorded items before the programme and make sure that you can hear the word cue. It may be muffled in background noise or not clearly delivered, in which case listen out for another cue or arrange with the director to have a different form of cueing. If it's a live insert to the programme, ask the director what the final question will be or what the 'out text' (the handover back to you) is – '. . . and that's it from Cape Town. Back to you, Amanda, in the studio.' Finally, always be aware of how you word your links in and out of VTs (*see* also pp. 87–93).

The Cue Light (Tally Light)

This is the light on top of the camera, which turns red when the camera is on-line – in other words, when the picture the camera is focusing on is being selected by the director for transmission or recording. It's activated by the vision mixer or director cutting to that camera. Other cameras may be focusing on the same picture, but if their picture is not being selected then their light will be off.

Sometimes you will be asked to take your cue from the camera light switching on to red: the director may say, 'Take your cue from camera 2.' In time it becomes a matter of habit to know which camera has its light on. But, as mentioned above, if you have been directed or cued to a camera that has its light off, do as you are told. It may be an artistic decision; if it was a mistake, the director will soon shout in your ear or the floor manager will jump up and down, directing you to face the correct camera.

Cue lights around or behind the set

Fixed to the scenery, these are used from behind the set to cue someone who doesn't have a direct sight of the action or cannot hear the verbal cue. More often than not an assistant floor manager will stand with that person and cue them, but it's as well to be aware of those cue lights. Usually it's just one red light which flashes on as the cue to go. If there are two lights, check with the floor manager which is your cue. In some instances a single flash of red is the cue to go, and sometimes it's a cue to stand by (or to be ready to go) – and then green is go! No matter how many times you've done it, don't assume you already know the procedure. Every occasion is different and there may be new technicians in the studio with their own methods. Check and double check. Just imagine what it would be like to make a premature entrance.

Hand cues

These are given to the presenter by the floor manager. They should be clean and precise. If you haven't worked with the floor manager before, check that you both recognise the same signals: although the fundamental signs should be the same, each floor manager has their own style. Be absolutely confident that you understand each sign that you will be given, and make sure you can see the floor manager out of the corner of your eye. If you can't, ask them to move to a position where they are in your eyeline but not in the camera's vision.

As well as giving you a signed hand cue, the floor manager may vocalise the count. That could be directly before transmission, coming out of a commercial break back into the programme, or cueing out of a VT recording. *The last 5 seconds of that count will always be SILENT, and so should you be.* This is a safeguard in the event of the studio sound or your own mic being faded up early. If that happens, it's possible the viewer may hear either the floor manager counting or a bit of gossip you didn't want to spread to the nation. It is also a useful 5 seconds which you can use to refocus on the programme itself.

EXERCISES

These are simple exercises to help you listen and talk at the same time.

(1) Tune into a radio news channel or talk show and listen to it through headphones or an earpiece. At the same time read aloud an item of news, preferably a piece you've never read before. Record your efforts on audio cassette or video and when you replay it, observe the strength of your concentration. Did you remain involved and interested in the item you were presenting?

(2) Choose any topic to talk about for 3 or 4 minutes. Give your friend a stopwatch and ask them to cut in at any time after a minute of your chat and give you a 30-second warning to finish. Then to cut in with a 15-second warning. At 10 seconds to the finish your friend should count down clearly from 10 seconds to 1 second . . . and cut.
Practise this a few times and then tape yourself, either on audio cassette or video. You'll be able to judge just how well you cope with instructions.
Once you can do it with ease you can ask your friend to throw in more instructions. For example: carry on for another 10 seconds; mention the window box; don't forget it's Maria's birthday. How smoothly did you incorporate the new information?

HAND CUE PRACTICE

(1) In front of a mirror, practise the hand cues illustrated below as if you were the floor manager. You will see then how they should look.

(2) Ask your friend to join you and practise them together. Choose a magazine or news item lasting about a minute and ask your friend to time you. As you reach 30 seconds your friend can then signal appropriately how much time you have left, again at 15 seconds and then a countdown from 10 to 1 and cue.

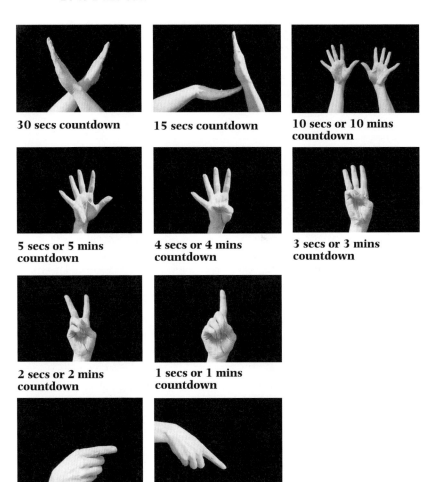

30 secs countdown

15 secs countdown

10 secs or 10 mins countdown

5 secs or 5 mins countdown

4 secs or 4 mins countdown

3 secs or 3 mins countdown

2 secs or 2 mins countdown

1 secs or 1 mins countdown

and cue

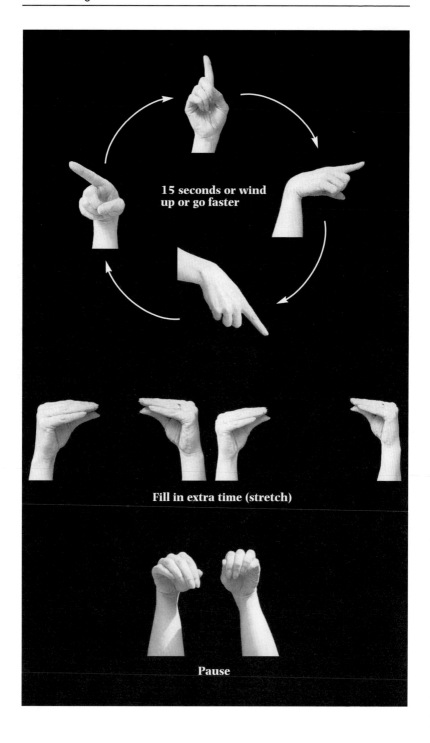

15 seconds or wind up or go faster

Fill in extra time (stretch)

Pause

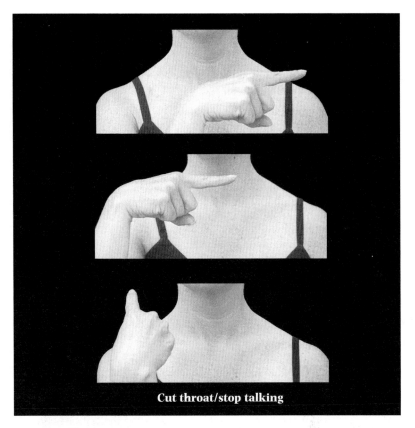

Cut throat/stop talking

Make sure that you are looking straight ahead as if you were looking into a camera lens. Your friend should *not* be in your direct eyeline, but slightly to one side or under where the camera would be. This will help you to be more aware of your peripheral vision.

(3) Select a topic to talk on for a minute or two and repeat the last exercise. This time ask your friend to use any of the other hand cues, including: go faster; wind up; fill in extra time (*stretch*); pause.

10

The Teleprompt

Known in the trade as the 'autocue' or 'autoscript', this suspicious piece of technology can be your very best friend. When you don't have to remember what you want to say and, in theory, when you have no need for cue cards or sheets of notes, the teleprompt should leave you to concentrate on a clean, clear, direct presentation. All this is true, but some presenters take advantage of its convenience and use it as an excuse not to rehearse or practise their links in and out of programme items. This is foolhardy as well as lazy. You still need to read through your script and practise.

If it is possible, read the script aloud with the prompt operator, even if it's only the opening and closing lines. It will help you to accustom your eyes to reading from the screen and regulate a speed at which you can read comfortably. Quite often the operator themselves will ask you to do this; be obliging. After all, you will be working together and it is for your benefit – in fact, you are likely to be very reliant on them. Introduce yourself, let them see your face. For the duration of the show they'll be watching a computer screen, not you, and it's good for them to have a face to match the voice. If you are unused to reading from a speaker prompt, find as many opportunities as you can to have a go, and rehearse reading aloud the whole of your text from the screen if you can. Once you become familiar with the skill, you will relax and be a far more fluent presenter. If it looks as though you are obviously reading from the prompt, you will alienate your audience. Ideally, you should read with ease whilst continuing to talk and look as though you are speaking directly to the viewer.

THE PROMPT SCREENS

The prompt screens can be placed almost anywhere that they are required. For TV presenting purposes the text is transmitted on to a mini screen mounted underneath the camera, and reflected on to a glass which is fixed directly over the camera lens itself. At business conferences the script is often transmitted to a monitor set in the lectern desk from

Teleprompt operator

which the presenter can read, or alternatively then projected on to two glasses set at angles on the lectern, on the right- and left-hand sides of the speaker. You'll see these most commonly used at conferences where the speakers need to keep their faces lifted as they address the audience. For live awards shows or big variety events, the text is sometimes transmitted to several large monitors suspended above and behind the audience's heads or fixed on to a theatre's circle trim. This gives the director freedom to take camera shots from the auditorium with no cameras on stage. The skilled presenter will give the impression of having no visual aids and use the opportunity to move freely, including the audience and roving cameras in their performance rather than fixing on one monitor. It is important to take time to incorporate the live audience in your presentation as well as the audience at home. Both parties know the score and will accept your divided focus. It's a balance you need to find for yourself as appropriate for each particular event, so that neither the audience nor the viewer feels excluded.

Sometimes the script is transmitted on to monitors placed on the floor at the front of the stage or presenting area. These are also known as 'outriders'. To use these effectively, make glances down at the prompt screen part of your natural movement. The same principles of reading the prompt apply at live events and theatre. Be natural. Be relaxed.

READING FROM THE PROMPT

The text of your script is typed on to a computer with a printout and disc available should you need them. The text is then transmitted to all the screens connected to the computer. The script that is given to the operator will be the one that appears before you, with all the punctuation, underlining, capital letters and so on that you and the director or PA have detailed. If you are sharing with a co-presenter, get their agreement before you change the layout of the prompt script. You may wish to insert double line spacing between each paragraph so that each new thought is clearly defined and marked on the script; this stops you from reading-on in a hurry. Naturally, you will take a breath between paragraphs and read from your script with renewed energy.

Prior to transmission, changes may be made to the script at any time. You may wish to change the odd word so that it reads better for you, or add cue notes to yourself – e.g. pause; smile; slow down; turn to watch video, etc. You can ask the operator to underline or put in capitals the words that you think require extra emphasis. It's also possible to separate difficult words and phonetically spell difficult names. However, be economical – don't litter the script with these personal memos or you may distract yourself, interrupting the flow of your presentation. It's your script; use it to make your performance work. If you have changes to make, try to do them all at once and so keep the operator as a friend. And, most importantly, check *all* changes you want to make with the director and co-presenter, since everyone is working from the same script.

Read what is there, don't make it up. If you do you'll get lost, and the director, producer, vision mixer and PA won't know what's going on either. Consequently there will be confusion when it's time to cue VTs, graphics and plotted camera shots. The exception to this is if a VT fails to run or some other mishap occurs that necessitates you covering or ad libbing (*see* also pp. 100–2). However, if you do intend to deviate from the agreed script – and you'd better have a very good reason – let the prompt operator and the director know where you are going to do this to avoid a mild panic during transmission. If you suddenly get a flash of inspiration to ad lib, indicate this to the operator, the director and the viewer by saying, 'I'd like to take a moment to tell you of an incident. . . .' or 'It's just occurred to me that . . .,' etc. The operator will then stop, and when you go back to the text you can pick up the script from where you left off. There have been many instances when a presenter has strayed from the script and the prompt operator, thinking that the presenter has leapt ahead to a new item, begins scrolling through looking for the text. All the presenter sees then is their script literally flying past before their eyes in front of the camera lens.

Texts can be made bigger or smaller depending on your vision and how far the camera is away from you. Check this for yourself with the operator, and make sure you can see your words clearly. The director may get a close up of you from 20 ft (6 metres) but from that distance you may find it difficult to read the prompt. Too far away and you'll be stretching your neck forwards and peering; too close and you'll find it difficult to focus. Sometimes a camera operator or floor manager will ask you what works best for you. Experiment. Don't be afraid of asking the prompt operator to change the size of the text or of discussing the camera position with the floor manager to see if it can be changed. If you have a co-presenter you will need to come to a mutual agreement, or at least warn them that your sections of the script will be slightly larger or smaller. Remain attentive when you are co-presenting – after all, you are sharing this news – and do not shuffle any sheets of script when your partner is in vision. If you wear reading glasses, have them on before you start!

Sometimes there is a marker, such as an arrow or a line dash, in the left-hand margin, to show you which line you are currently reading. This marker can be moved so that it appears at the top, middle or bottom of the screen – wherever you prefer the line you are reading to be. There are two schools of thought on where to focus:

(1)   read the script as it reaches the centre of the screen
(2)   read the script as it reaches the top of the screen, the top line. However, too close to the top and the temptation is to speed up to prevent the words disappearing before you read them.

Personally, I like it to be a third or half-way down so that my eyeline and focus remain in the centre. It's a marginal difference and it's really up to you to find what is most comfortable for your read.

```
The text is written in columns
of five or six words, using
a courier font. It is important
that, when reading, you don't
stop or pause at the end of
each line but keep the momentum
of your thought flowing through to
the end of the sentence. Practise
reading newspaper items aloud, and
if you can obtain a copy of
your script from the prompt
operator to practise with and
read in advance, then this is
ideal.
```

The trick to reading from a teleprompt is to read 'through' the screen, through to the TV camera lens. The commonest mistake is to move your head along with your eyes as you read line by line. Keep your neck relaxed so that any head movement you make is natural and free. Keep a natural quality to your voice, varying pitch and some pace. Remember that although you have the words in front of you, you still need to make contact with the viewer and deliver your script with commitment.

The pace of the script scrolling up from the bottom of the screen is dictated by the presenter. If you speed up, slow down or even stop, so will the pace of the script – as the operator is following you. When you recommence, so will the operator.

PRESENTER-DRIVEN TELEPROMPT

This is fast becoming a common apparatus for news readers. It's cheaper because fewer people need to be employed – no prompt operator, no camera operator, no floor manager, no PA. Just you, the director and the duty engineer, and maybe someone from sound and lighting – maybe!

Your script is typed on to the computer by you, or one of your colleagues if you are sharing the workload. Most companies using this method have a pre-formatted computer programme where each item is titled and cued-up alongside any VT inserts and interviews. This is to assist the director with cueing. (You will have an earpiece and will be in constant contact with the production gallery.) In the studio your computer should be linked to the local computer network. And so long as the computer programme is open and not 'read only', it will allow you to search for or skip items, revise or edit text. Remember to keep the director informed of any changes. Depending on the set design, the keyboard could be set into, or placed on, the presenter's desk. With all the hardware connected, the script appears on the screen over the camera lens. Without an operator it's up to you to run the speaker prompt.

Currently there are three modes of driving:

- the foot pedal
- the hand pressure control
- the hand wheel.

The foot pedal
This operates like a car accelerator pedal and similarly you need to familiarise yourself with its response. The harder you press the pedal, the faster the script rolls up the screen. You are in control. To begin with you might like to consider wearing shoes with soles that are not too thick so that you can be sensitive to the pressure required. Test it out each time you come to transmission. On the pedal box is a red button: depressing it dictates forward or reverse roll for when you need to go back in the script during rehearsal or a retake.

Hand pressure control
This works in much the same way as the foot pedal. It's more convenient for the presenter when standing, but you may find that it restricts your hand movements.

Hand wheel

This is attached to a small box and needs to be turned to move the text. It limits camera shots and can easily be knocked during an interview or during a VT insert if you haven't locked it off into position. In such an event you may well lose your place in the script. The hand wheel also limits the use of your hands.

WHAT HAPPENS IF THE PROMPT BREAKS DOWN?

Firstly, don't panic! If the show is not transmitting live, the director will stop the recording and you can all start again. During a live broadcast it may be just a glitch and the text will come back soon. There may even be a back-up system – ask the operator beforehand. To help you out of any difficulties carry some notes or cue cards, or give them to the floor manager. Alternatively, make sure a hard copy of the script is some-where on the set (but be sure to tell the floor manager where it is before transmission, in case they 'tidy up'!). Whether using a script or cue cards, glance up to the camera regularly to keep eye contact with the viewer and an eye open for when the teleprompt is running again.

'Always have a hard copy with you. Sometimes I just laugh if it goes down.'
Lisa Aziz (Sky News, BBC)

'We depend on it so much! It's really important to keep your script in order: the one evening the prompt goes down will be the day your hard copy is all over the place.'
Jeremy Vine (BBC Newsnight)

'Do I tell the viewer?'

This depends entirely on the programme. News readers don't have the time and they will more than likely have hard copy scripts in front of them. In a lighthearted magazine programme it's more appropriate to explain to the viewer what is going on – a breakdown is every presenter's worst nightmare so it may even be fun to share the setback. They will understand, feel that they're part of the show, and it may even add a little drama and spontaneity: 'Well it's happened, and it's happened to me – the prompt has gone down, so please bear with us whilst we see what can be done,' or 'Just a moment. I do apologise, we have a slight technical hitch. I'll go back to my original notes.'

Whatever you do, don't hang about. It is your job to cover. You can be sure that you won't be the only one whose heart has missed a beat and everything will be being done to get the system back up. You just keep going. Talk to your friend, the viewer. Keep them interested. Tell them what's coming up next, move on to a new topic – just get on with the show. Don't lose your temper or make a sour jibe at the production team, it is rude. The majority of viewers will be aware that behind the scenes, everyone is working very hard to get things back to normal and you will be the one who comes off looking like an idiot. Remain in control, don't try to bluff. Be honest and everyone will admire your professionalism.

IN SUMMARY

- Check any changes you have made or wish to make to your script with the director or floor manager.
- Make sure that your script matches the teleprompt script. Have a hard copy of your script close at hand.
- Relax your neck and shoulders.
- Keep your head up, and your voice and all movements natural.
- Check that you can see the text clearly.
- If you wear spectacles, have them on before you start.
- Rehearse some lines aloud.
- Set a steady reading pace.
- If you are using a self-driven prompt, test all the equipment.
- Read 'through' the screen, don't peer.
- Read through to the end of the sentence, not to the end of the line.
- You are using a prompt. You must still present with conviction and energy and give the impression of spontaneity.
- Be cool, calm and collected.
- When you can – practise, practise, practise.

'Get some studio experience. Some young presenters went for an audition and freaked out at all the technical skills required. Any natural qualities they had went out of the window. They'd never seen an autocue in their lives.'
Lance Goodwin (Presenters' agent)

11

Running Order and Script Layout

RUNNING ORDER

All programmes have a running order, and all departments get a copy in advance. Items and order can change but at least everyone starts with the same plan. Every director has their own individual way of setting out a running order and not all the information will apply to everyone. You have to decide what is useful to you.

Details on a running order usually include:

- item number
- description of item
- location/source/studio area
- expected duration of item (Dur.)
- expected or estimated accumulated running time (RX), to be updated by the PA during recording or transmission
- actual accumulated running time (TX), constantly updated by the PA during recording or transmission.

SCRIPT LAYOUT

Most scripts are laid out to a similar format. Details on the script may include the following:

- the spoken text written in a column on the right-hand side
- each item numbered on the script (Item 4; Item 5, etc.)
- location of the shot (Studio Area A, B, C)
- style of the shot (close up, wide shot)
- shot number (Shot 1; Shot 2)
- camera number involved in the shot (Cam 2, Cam 3)
- source of sound (VO, SOVT)
- person speaking (name of presenter or other)

Sample running order: news headlines

NO.	ITEM	SOURCE/AREA	DUR.	RX.	TX.
	A	B	C	D	E
1	OPENING TITLES	VT - 1	5"	5"	
2	PRESENTER INTRO	NEWS AREA - A	5"	10"	
3	NEWS TRAILER	VT2 + PRES. V/O	15"	25"	
4	LINK TO BRIDGE	NEWS AREA - A	10"	35"	
5	BRIDGE REPORT	VT - 1	30"	1'05"	
6	LINK TO HEAT WAVE	NEWS AREA - A	8"	1'13"	
7	HEAT WAVE REPORT	VT2 + PRES. V/O	10"	1'23"	
8	LINK TO VACCINE	NEWS AREA - A	7"	1'30"	
9	VACCINE REPORT	O.B.	25"	1'55"	
10	INTV. GUEST & PRES.	NEWS AREA - A	1'30"	3'25"	
11	LINK FASHION WEEK	NEWS AREA - A	5"	3'30"	
12	FASHION WK. REPORT	VT - 1	12"	4'42"	
13	LINK SPORTS	NEWS AREA - A	5'	4'47"	
14	SPORTS REPORT	ASTON + PRES.V/O	40"	5'27"	
15	LINK CHOCOLATE	NEWS AREA - A	6"	5'33"	
16	CHOCOLATE REPORT	VT - 2	10"	5'43"	
17	LINK TO 9:30 NEWS	NEWS AREA - A	5"	5'48"	
18	9:30 NEWS TRAILER	VT - 1 + PRES V/O	12"	6'	
19	GOODBYE	NEWS AREA - A	5"	6'05"	
20	CLOSING CREDITS	VT - 2	6"	6'11"	

Key: DUR - expected duration of item
      RX - expected accumulated running time
      TX - actual accumulated running time

- source of vision (VT, ASTON)
- basic information of VT or live links
- durations and cues.

When you get your script, make sure you do the following.

(1) Put your name on the top. It is then easier for everyone to know that it's yours, if you put it down.

(2) Read it.

(3) Make sure each new item on the running order corresponds with its number on the script and on the teleprompt.

(4) Ensure that each news item or new topic begins on a separate page. If it doesn't, mark each new item with a line or circle the item number.

(5) Identify which parts of the script are yours and mark them either with a highlighter pen or with a thick black line down both sides of your words.

(6) Clearly mark names and words that are difficult to pronounce. If it helps, spell them out phonetically on your script or divide them up (e.g. multi-syl-lab-ic). Do the same on the teleprompt.

(7) Check the 'in' and 'out' words of any VTs and handovers to and from co-presenters and reporters.

(8) Mark any item on your script which ends with a 'hard count'. This might be to a commercial break or the end of the programme. Allowing for three spoken words per second, mark where the 5-second count can be expected to begin. Your marker will give you an indication of whether you need to cut or lengthen your script, or quicken or slow your pace so that you can finish in perfect time.

(9) Note down names of the crew with whom you may need to communicate. Technical staff – PA, vision mixer, sound engineer, camera operators, floor manager, director! Note down names of guests, reporters and co-presenters. When so much is going on, names can be the first thing to slip out of your mind.

At the back of the book is a formatted script exercise for you to practise – *see* pp. 191-5.

12

Linking Items –
Ins and Outs

There are hundreds of different ways in which to begin and to end a programme. In between, you have introductory links (the 'ins' or 'intros') to VT, guest interviews, outside broadcasts, news reports, weather, business, demonstrations, commercial breaks . . . the list goes on. And of course you have the 'outs' or 'outros' on those items too.

A basic programme format comprises:

- intro – welcome to the show, what's in store
- middle – the programme
- outro – a recap of the show, farewell to the guests if relevant, and a look ahead to the next programme. A final goodbye.

These tips apply equally to live-event presentation, where the host must link from speaker to interview to video report to awards. Wherever you are presenting, the director will require you to stick to the script when it comes to intros and outros. This is for technical reasons: they will have plotted on their script (amongst other directions) exactly where they intend to change a camera shot and where the countdown to a VT begins. You cannot just abruptly change the script with no warning, since you'll be the one left, in vision, looking like a fool. In any event, all text changes should be checked, because scripts are frequently written to comply with production or legal restraints.

INS (INTROS)

Most programmes begin with a welcome. So do just that – welcome your audience. There's a current trend not to start the programme with a greeting such as, 'Hello' or 'Good morning' but rather to launch straight into the script. If that's how your programme starts, then put a 'Hello' in your voice – start with an unspoken welcome. If you don't, the viewer may subconsciously feel that you have started without them and that they are an unwelcome guest at your party. Great, if that's what's intended, but don't be surprised if they leave the party for one where they feel more involved!

There are many distractions for today's viewer, and many channels to choose from. It's important that your opening lines and image should be clean and direct, and seize people's attention from the beginning. Start *on* the voice, do not warm up as you go. Time spent pre-studio on vocal exercises will help, as of course will plenty of rehearsal. Remember that you can always do some preliminary vocal warm-up exercises in the car or in your dressing room.

If you're working on a network TV programme, be careful of 'regionalising'. For instance, if it's warm and sunny where you are, check the weather for the whole of your broadcasting area. Folk in a snow blizzard won't want to hear you going on about how everyone is having a glorious day. Remember who your audience is, and where it is, too.

LINKS

Links form a bridge from topic to topic. When you are introducing guests, fellow presenters or the next topic, keep your vocal inflection up at the end of the sentence. In this way you carry the viewer's interest with you into the next section. If you are passing over to someone else in the studio, it's generally good manners to refer to them: '. . . and now back to Joel.' (*Turn* to look at Joel!) It's common practice to find a connection between each item, but if the link is too tenuous you can always make a joke of it or say, 'And now for something completely different.'

Try to change your tone with the mood of each topic. A cosy, friendly approach to the naming of a new rose may lead very neatly into a report on horse manure, but since the two are quite different subjects you will need to show that in your voice. Visualise the subject you are talking about (*see* also Chapter 4, *Using Your Voice Effectively*) and anticipate the mood-change if you can. It's your responsibility to lead the audience smoothly from item to item. Bear in mind that contrasting reports often follow each other, and the transition should be sensitive and inoffensive. For instance, a serious news report on a fatal train crash might be followed by a light-hearted report of a snake that can sing the National Anthem – take care with such severe 'gear changes'. Live magazine shows are very often interspersed with news bulletins. The general rule is to keep up the momentum and character of your own programme unless the news is unusually serious, in which case take advice from your producer. To practise varying news items and assorted lists of topics coming up in a programme, there are exercises at the end of this chapter for you to try.

Links in and out of VT

Make sure you give all videos a clear introduction. VTs are cued to run from an 'instant start': this means that as soon as the director hears the verbal cue, the video will start. The director needs the cue to be clear. Don't fluster if it doesn't run immediately, just wait and keep quiet. If nothing has happened after 5 seconds, and you have received no further instruction via your earpiece or via the floor manager, then you can recover the situation with an ad lib and move on to the next item.

If possible, watch the VT before the programme. You may want to include some reference to it in your link into it or before the next item. Listen to the verbal intros and outros so that you don't speak the video script – i.e. 'And now over to James in Bulgaria' as the VT begins 'Hello, I'm James and I'm in Bulgaria'. This is called a duplicate link and the viewer will think either that you haven't been watching, or that you believe they're stupid and need to be told twice. Either way they won't be impressed.

Find out how the VT ends, for although you may have a floor manager counting you back to the live camera, you don't want to be surprised by any sudden or unanticipated endings. At the end of your intro, turn towards the monitor – this gives the impression that you are watching the VT with the viewer and sharing the experience. The same applies when handing over to someone else in another studio. 'Joining us from the inquiry is our reporter Megan Falconer.' *Turn.* 'Hello Megan. What's the latest news?' If you are watching a VT, use the last lines to cue yourself to turn: for example, 'The swans were last seen in Rye.' *Turn* back to camera. It's not essential to repeat this move at every link; you will need to judge where and if it's appropriate for the next item. You or the producer may, for instance, want to start the next item direct to the camera, without any physical or verbal reference to the last item. Vary the moves, always remembering to be sensitive to the viewer. Talk to them, be their guide. As long as you've been paying attention, you'll be able to link out of a VT with ease, sensitively picking up its mood and then changing it accordingly.

Links to commercial break

These are really important. You want the audience to stay tuned to your show and channel, and your bosses most certainly do. Let the viewer know what's coming up after the break or entice them in some way to stay. Intrigue them. Just think what they'll miss if they leave now! Technically, you need to keep the life and energy in your voice: it needs to carry the programme and viewers through the commercial break to the next segment, which is quite a long time. So whatever you say and however you say it, make it count.

In a live show you will be counted back into the programme after a commercial break. Whether it's a live transmission or not, pick up the programme with the same enthusiasm. The viewer has been deluged with visual marketing and taken far away from the experience of your programme, so welcome them back. Remind them what's going on.

OUTS – AT THE END OF THE PROGRAMME

You're on the home stretch now, and quite naturally your inner voice is preparing for 'time out'. Not yet! Keep that energy going and keep the enthusiasm flowing. You may wish to summarise what they've seen and if you know, indicate what happens next. It's usual to be counted out of the programme by the director, the PA and/or the floor manager – usually from one minute, with signals at 30 seconds, 15 seconds and then a count from 10 seconds to zero. Whilst part of your brain should be conscious of this and attentive to their instructions, the rest of you must keep the pace of the programme alive and not slide down to a 'muddy' finish.

End clearly and cleanly

At the end of the programme it's acceptable to start tidying up your desk and your props, sorting out your script or putting away your pen. However, make sure it's part of the filmed action. Do not actually finish, pack up and leave until the floor manager or PA tells you that you are off-air or that recording has stopped.

EXERCISES – LINKS

(1) Watch a magazine programme – especially the morning programmes, which deal with a variety of subjects – and see how they list the items which will be featured. This is called a *menu* and it's presented as a taster for the show.

(2) Now compile a list of items to be featured in the programme which you would like to present (or use the ones below). Link them together to form a 45-second read. Record yourself on audio cassette or video.
Was there a difference between items? Would you be interested in any those items as you presented them? How well did you use your voice?

Local news
Little girl found safe and well.
House roof blows off.
New film-house opens.
Hospital health and safety concerns.
How to write a song – local songwriter tells all.

Saturday morning
Boy band interview.
The Cabbage Soup Game.
Internet questions answered.
Hurley and Burley cartoon.
Skateboarding quest.
Create your own jungle.

Sports programme
5-a-side local football.
Sumo wrestling.
Mountain bike racing in America.
Preparing for the competition day.

Holiday
Reports from Marrakesh and Copenhagen.
Emma at the Moscow Ballet.
Jo at the Great Barrier Reef, Australia.
John re-visits Valetta in Malta.

Foreign correspondent
Living after an earthquake.
Floods in India – climatic changes.
Genocide weapons traced back to the UK.
A new Hong Kong.
Human Rights update.

EXERCISES – LINKS TO VT

It's common practice to put each item and accompanying VT details on a seperate page of script. Here I've put them on the same page. Practise reading these scripts with energy and conviction as if you were linking to a live VT.

(shot) 9. Cam. 1 MCU PRES. STUDIO	/

ITEM 15 LINK TO VT DIY

Presenter   We seem to be inundated with DIY programmes suggesting that you can change the look of your house, flat, garage or garden. It certainly has been the latest craze of 'things to do'. *But*, what extra expenses can you incur? What real value are you adding or deducting? Have you got planning permission? Do you need planning permission?

10. VT – 2	/

ITEM 16 DIY		SOVT

    IN WORDS:
    VISUAL – BUILDER ON ROOF HAMMERING
    DUR: 00.45
    OUT WORDS: '. . . I'll know better next time.'
    Out Vis. – Heap of rubble

(shot) 13. Cam. 1 MCU PRES. STUDIO	/

ITEM 10 LINK TO VT BADMINTON INTERVIEW

Presenter   A chance now to catch up on the finals of the English National Badminton Championships, where Ben Moult is aiming for his 10th victory of the year. However, the rising star Vincent Danson from Birkenhead is likely to prove a strong challenger. Suzanne Jackson caught up with him earlier today.

14. VT – 1	/

ITEM 11 BADMINTON INTERVIEW	SOVT

    IN WORDS: 'This may look like an ordinary shuttlecock . . .'

OUT WORDS: . . . 'Good luck Vincent, we look
forward to this afternoon's match.'
Out Vis. – Vincent smiling

17. CAM. 1 MCU. PRES. STUDIO   /

ITEM 14 LINK TO VT PHOTOS
Presenter   Did two girls really photograph fairies at the bottom
of the garden? Their story still remains as
controversial as ever, as do many unusual images
of so called UFOs. How can you fell the fact from
the fiction when such sophisticated photographic
equipment is now used?
Last week scientists and photographers got together
and came up with some surprising new evidence.
Tim James reports.

18. VT – 1   /

ITEM 15 PHOTOS   SOVT
IN WORDS: 'Take these two pictures. . .'
DUR: 1:32
OUT WORDS: '. . . I guess seeing is believing.'
Out Vis. – Starry sky

Suggested VT titles for you to link:

● Investing £1000
● The Royal Opera House
● Motorbike trails
● A day with the Miami Police team
● Oyster fishing in the Gambia
● Teddy bear collections.

13

Handling Objects

Inanimate objects can reduce the most competent presenters to tears. They are the stuff of nightmares and the material for humorous out-takes. If it can go wrong, it will, and you have to be prepared for every eventuality. The popular advice is to have total respect for the object you intend to handle and treat it with great care. With practice it can become your friend rather than something to fear, because as your focus of attention centres on the object or demonstration, any nervous tension you have will ebb away. Objects are a useful standby when filling in time or thinking about what comes next. Children's presenters can be seen chatting away to cuddly bunnies whilst racking their brains trying to remember forgotten lines. An egg-whisk can become an interesting feature in the kitchen as the TV chef waits for a cake to rise. So, don't be scared of objects. Even when a potted plant develops a life of its own, be in control. It's not always necessary to let the viewer know about every mistimed detail unless something happens that is apparent to everyone – in which case, laugh and share your dilemma. It's no good lying or bravely covering up. More than likely the viewer will be enjoying the 'cock-up', so you might as well involve them. After all, what's the harm in being seen to be human. Relax and take command.

Bear in mind that when the camera rolls, objects that have behaved themselves during rehearsals sometimes do exactly the opposite! It's essential to familiarise yourself with their every detail beforehand.

PREPARATION

It doesn't matter how large or small an item, or whether it's automated or inert, get to know everything about it. Most of this is common sense, but it's worth reminding you to read the operating instructions thoroughly. Read any booklets which give you extra tips or related information on an object's use and purpose. Ask anyone who has knowledge or expertise for their input. Give yourself a safety net by preparing what you are going to say if the technology or gadget doesn't work.

Check-list

Obviously, not all the following checks will be necessary – select the relevant ones and test them out thoroughly.

- Test out each working button and lever.
- Locate the ON switch and, very importantly, the OFF switch.
- If it opens and closes, how does it do so?
- Are there any surprise knobs or keys? Is there a lock you should know about?
- Try lifting the item. How much does it weigh?
- Are there any surprise noises, alarms or bleeps?
- How long does it run for? Is there any way of cutting off the sound or shutting it down before its programme drive has finished?
- How delicate is it? How vigorous can you be with it? Can you touch it at all?
- Is it hot or cold?
- What does it taste like?
- Is it slippy or sticky?

It is not only objects you will be handling that need care, but anything you will be coming into contact with – pieces of scenery, statues, clothes rails, chairs. Test everything out. Will it support your weight? Can you lean on it? If you put your hand on a Lego man's head made of 1000 pieces, as Blue Peter presenter Mark Curry did, will it fall off?

SHOWING THE OBJECT TO THE CAMERA

Inert objects

The camera shot will be framed on the object for a big close-up (BCU). Every movement you make, therefore, should be precise and slowed down to less than half-speed, letting each adjustment be caught by the camera. Turn the item deliberately. Plan a logical 'route' around the object rather than hopping from one side to another. Just a slight tilt and the item can slip out of shot; use the output monitor to reassure yourself that the object is in the frame and to correct any movements you make.

The camera has to fix on the item you are talking about so don't wave it about – or to the viewer it will just be a blur. If your guest, the expert, is waving the item about, take it off them, politely saying something like, 'If I may, I'll just hold it still for those at home.' Make your hands a stand for the object and let it rest on them whilst you talk. To stop your hands from swaying about or shaking, try tucking your elbows into your waist. When pointing out a particular feature, keep your finger still, since even the tiniest movement framed in close-up can be distracting. Fragile articles require an even more delicate touch. Be sure you know how to hold it and how it moves. Identify which bits are likely to fall off! With very small, detailed objects you can use a pointer to draw attention to individual features. Big and wide fingers can obliterate tiny details and so a cocktail stick or needlework stitch-holder can prove a practical alternative. Big hands look better if the palms face inwards. And remember to scrub clean your hands and nails.

Now for the tricky bit. When you are displaying the item to the camera, it will appear to be upside down to you – as will any writing or instructions. The objective is to offer the object to the camera rather than looking at it yourself which cuts out the viewer. It's an open, outward movement. Prior to recording, practise this unnatural demonstration. Be aware of the direction of each move. The image seen on the monitor or on the TV set at home is not a mirror image of your action but a reverse reflection. Up and down movements are not affected, but sideways motion takes a bit of getting used to. (Technology is currently being developed to flip the picture to assist the presenter.)

Written notices
Cards, book and CD covers, any literature you want the viewer to read, must be held still. Let the camera focus on the sign and give the viewer time to read it.

DEMONSTRATIONS

When you hit the start button it will either (a) start and work as it should, (b) not start at all, (c) start and work but not in the way that it is expected to, or (d) explode. If it doesn't work in rehearsal, don't attempt to do it on air – that is, unless you and the producer or director have allowed for that as a part of the programme. If you've rehearsed and seen how it should work successfully, you'll very soon recognise if something is going wrong before the catastrophe happens. Once you've thoroughly checked the workings of the gadget, think of all the ways in which it might go wrong, and approach it from that angle: it won't work; it will spurt hot water at you; it won't stop; it's not compatible with the attachments. Then work out how you will cover if the worst does occur. Don't lose your temper with it, it won't sort out the problem any quicker. Take your time, think what else you can do, and keep talking using your research knowledge. Because you are demonstrating to the camera it might be easier to turn the object at an angle to you and try to make it work in a position more comfortable to yourself. If all else fails, tell the viewer how it *should* have worked. Hopefully the director will frame you in a close-up so that you can lose the errant object and move on to something else.

Any demonstration should be performed as a step-by-step procedure, slowly and methodically. This slows you down, giving you time to consider what next to say and do, and gives the camera operator a chance to focus and adjust the shot. You can also signal to the director what you are going to do next by talking your way through what you are doing. 'If I just lift up this side of the box . . . (*pause*) . . . you can see how ornately decorated it is.'

Demonstrating usually requires you to perform the action towards you. Cooking, for instance, would look very strange reversed towards the camera. Nevertheless, you will need to let the camera in and hold the frying pan still for a second or two for a clear picture. Erecting a construction requires practice and more concentration than you might apply if you were doing this for yourself at home. The skill is making it look easy, but not doing a rough, botched job. The professionals you see on TV DIY shows have worked out what they need to do beforehand – how many screws are required and which tools are needed – and ensured that all objects are within easy reach. If there's a complicated bit, then pause. Explain what you are about to do and then let the camera film the action. It's much better to get it right and add music or a voice-over later.

Fire and water

In rehearsal you should have discovered how much flame or liquid is needed. *Keep to that* and don't be tempted to experiment. Stand back from flames and if you are in any doubt at all, share your concerns with the floor manager and support crew. Ask them to stand by with safety equipment. Electricity is famously unreliable: take every precaution. Liquids go everywhere so add a few drops at a time. Don't splash it about unless the floor manager has given you the go-ahead to do so. Studio floors are extremely expensive and without the appropriate covering can easily be damaged. More importantly there are electricity cables and sensitive equipment all about you. For your own safety be advised by the floor manager. The same applies for outside broadcasts. Although it's easy to relax and have fun away from what can be a constrained studio environment, remember that there are live cables all around.

The patter

Be careful of what you say about an object. Firstly, is it true? Don't claim something can do things if it can't. It will rarely be the 'best product on the market', but you can say, 'In my opinion . . .', 'Research shows . . .', 'It is believed by experts to be . . .'. Be sure of your facts and beware of absolutes.

Having slowed down the action there is a danger of slowing down the speech so that it sounds patronising. Try to separate the rhythm of the action and the pace of your speech.

Reminder

All the above advice applies equally to your script, since it, too, is an object to be handled. Staple or clip the pages together securely (unless you are reading the news). If you are live on air and they scatter over the studio floor, or get caught in a gust of wind during an outside broad-cast, the next shot might be of you chasing script pages and then trying to sort them back into order!

EXERCISES

(1) Tune into any of the DIY programmes or shopping channels to watch the myriad 'dos and don'ts'. You can see what works and what doesn't and it will give you an insight into how to handle objects in a very short time.

(2) Set up a table with a camera focusing on your hands – a shot that frames you from the waist up, and the table.

(3) *'Show and tell'* – in this exercise the objective is to indicate relevant features on an inanimate article.
Choose items that have some detail on them, such as a shoe, a doll or a watch. Examine them carefully before you start.
Prepare what you want to say, giving yourself a time limit of 2 minutes.
Practise first without being recorded. Note every visual aspect.
Record and play back. Notice how a small, meaningless movement can be very distracting.

(4) Find a picture book, preferably a children's guide. An illustrated handbook will also suffice. Read it carefully. Get a good grasp of what the book is about and pay particular attention to the pictures. Present the closed book to camera, introduce the book and then open the first page.
Slowly turn each page, explaining what is in each picture and pointing out details where you think necessary. Video

this and watch your efforts. How much could you see upside down? Did your finger obscure anything important?

(5) *Demonstration* – the suggestions for experimenting are endless, but try one from each of the following categories:

    (a) *Technical/mechanical*
         Demonstrate how to use a camera.
         Demonstrate how to use a swiss army pen knife.

    (b) *DIY*
         Re-potting a plant.
         Making a sandwich.

    (c) *Fire and water*
         Create a floating candle table arrangement.
         Make a cocktail drink.

IN SUMMARY

- Assume that anything that *can* go wrong *will* go wrong.
- Prepare: use the check-list (*see* p. 95).
- Enforce step-by-step procedures, and do it slowly.
- Rehearse.
- Be sure of your facts.
- Talk to the viewers.
- Let the camera see what you are doing.

WHAT THEY SAY

'A shopping channel presenter has to go out there and deal with everything for 4 hours, live on TV. They don't have scripts or autocue – preparation is all. Presenters are encouraged to look at everything. Every move has to be in slow motion as if you are working in treacle. Be yourself and have fun. I was showing a wonderful ornate crystal bell which I picked up and rang. It smashed to a thousand pieces! I just accepted it and laughed; people still phoned in to buy the rest of the collection.'
Paul Lavers (producer and presenter of the Ideal Home Shopping Channel)

14

Coping with Technical Breakdowns

Although you hope they'll never happen, technical breakdowns are not infrequent. In fact, it's a credit to the professionalism of most TV presenters that the viewer doesn't pick up on them more often. The ability to handle the moment when things go wrong is often described by presenters as 'swimming serenely like a swan, whilst frantically paddling under the water'.

A breakdown may be caused by any technical fault, such as a VT failing to run, an outside broadcast link breaking up, a satellite link picture connecting with no sound, or even a guest not turning up. Whatever the problem, it's your job to make it appear that the programme is running smoothly. This requires you to be unflappable and thoroughly prepared. It calls on your skills as an able host and friend of the viewer to remain in control, even if you don't know what's going on. Listen carefully to the director's instructions and be ready to move swiftly on to the next item. If the director calls in your ear to 'read on', do just that (of course, this means knowing what is coming next in the programme). If you are waiting for a VT to run and it doesn't do so immediately, wait 5 seconds. Then, if it still doesn't run, get on with the show. If you have time and the programme format allows, briefly explain to the viewers and apologise – they'll feel part of the crisis, and be interested to see what happens next and how you'll get out of it! If the teleprompt goes down, use the hard copy, retaining eye contact with the viewer at all times. 'Always ensure that you've got hard copies, and if all else fails talk to your co-presenter,' Sophie Raworth (BBC *Breakfast News*) advises. 'Keep a conversation going between you.'

Some sample links
'I'm sorry, we seem to have lost that item so we'll move on.'
'As you can see we're having trouble with that particular link-up. We're trying to re-establish contact, so in the meantime . . .'
'We appear to have a technical problem. As soon as the fault is rectified we'll return to Westminster for the rest of that report.'

BACK-UP OR STANDBY SCRIPTS

It's a good idea to have a standby script which you can extend or cut as time dictates. It's better to have something you can read from or refer to, than to be left with the director shouting in your ear, 'Fill for 30 seconds' and to have nothing to say. Five seconds can seem an age, 30 seconds an eternity. If you are working in continuity, use a TV programme guide to help you. Be prepared to cut a standby script short as soon as normal programming resumes. Here's an example of a standby script:

'Due to a technical fault we've a slight delay to the start of the next programme. This does give me the opportunity to let you know what's in store this morning.

At 9.25 we're outward bound in Wales, as *Land and Legend* celebrates its magical rivers and waterfalls in poetry and prose. *The Body* examines our talented brain at 10 o'clock, and half an hour later our grey matter is given a full workout as Paul Spedding shows what it takes to become an astronaut. That's *Calling Planet Earth* at 10.30.

Back down to earth at 11 o'clock with a big bump: it's the *Sumo Boys of the Basho*. *The Millennium Mind* quiz follows at 12 noon and with *Daily Business* presented by Trish MacIntyre at 12.30, that's this morning's programmes here on TV 202.

I'm pleased to tell you that we can now go over to racing at Ascot.'

Alternatively you may wish to prepare a less generic script, one that is more relevant to your programme:

'While we're awaiting the arrival of Zoë George at the premiere of *The Place to Be*, here's a few interesting facts about the making of the film.

Eighteen thousand donuts were used in the famous kitchen scene, of which only 20 were eaten. Algar House has no back to it; in fact it's just a front facade. It rained four times during filming in the desert and we understand that Zoë begged to wear the skintight spacesuit which she wore in the film at tonight's premiere. We'll see if she got her wish. Yes, the car is just arriving. So it's back to Leicester Square . . .'

EXERCISES
(1)   Look up your TV guide and choose a link between two programmes. Imagine that the next programme doesn't run straight away.

Write a script to cover 30 seconds. Time yourself.
Then cut it to cover 15 seconds, 10 seconds and 5 seconds.

(2) Choose a specific programme that you would like to present. Invent a reason why there might be a break or delay *within* the programme, and write a covering script of 2 minutes, 1 minute and 30 seconds.

WHAT THEY SAY

'At some point the presenter will have to carry the show when nothing else is working. That's the moment at which you find out whether you are half-way good. It comes down to being relaxed and trying to keep thinking that this is very ordinary. That's when you earn your money – when it all goes wrong.'
Jeremy Vine (BBC Newsnight)

'If there's nothing on the autocue, no script in front of you and you hear the director say, 'Oh God' in your ear, then you know they've no idea what's going on either . . . and you're live on air. That to me is what you're paid for. When it's happening it's not actually frightening; it's when it's finished and you're wondering, 'What the hell was that' that reality kicks in. That sort of fright is manageable after time – being a professional means dealing with those fears.'
Simon McCoy (SKY News)

'There's no visual aid other than the monitor to show what you are talking about. If it goes wrong, everything is crazy with people shouting in your ear. That's where your training comes in, that's what you get paid for.'
Siân Lloyd (ITN Weather)

15

Interviewing

Asking questions is something we do every day of our lives. You want to know something, so you look for an answer. Interviewing on TV, therefore, should present no problem. But the constraints of time, an unnatural environment, and the fact that you are asking questions on behalf of the viewer rather than yourself, all contribute to making the job that much harder.

The TV interview is a three-way split between interviewer, viewer and interviewee, and is often referred to as a triangle of trust. In essence, each party trusts that the others will co-operate to provide the best possible interview for them.

THE INTERVIEWER

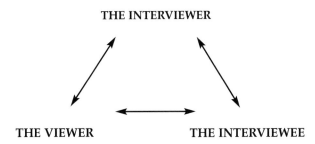

THE VIEWER   **THE INTERVIEWEE**

Figure 15.1 The Triangle of Trust

THE INTERVIEWER

An integral part of the presenter's job, interviewing is the skill of honing questions to obtain the most significant and interesting answers. As the interviewer, your task is to provide the viewer with information, interpretation and entertainment – and above all, to ask the questions you consider that the viewer would like answered. You need to be genuinely interested in someone else's point of view or experience. Be polite, be persistent and, when it's appropriate, have fun, joke and tease – but always be careful not to overstep the mark and become offensive.

Relationship with the viewer

Interviews only make good TV as long as the viewer is not left out of the discussion. If during your chat you make a reference to a previous personal contact (for example, reminiscing over the time you both met in Istanbul), be sure to tell the audience the bigger story. Otherwise, they'll resent the fact that you are having a private discussion and are not prepared to share your experiences. Clarify complicated answers and translate jargon. You might know what the guest is talking about, because you've done some research on the subject, but once again you need to consider the viewer.

Kirsty Lang believes that there is nothing too complicated that cannot be explained in simple terms. 'You may be given a script written by a highly specialised expert, but one that is quite difficult to understand. On TV you have to cover all bases. The key is not to do it in a patronising way: don't talk down, but explain it to a friend on your own level.'

Relationship with the interviewee

Some maintain that an interview is only as good as the interviewee. Their contribution is obviously vital, but the way in which the interviewer handles the exchange in order to draw out the most reticent individual requires both skill and professionalism. Somehow, you need to gain their trust – especially since most people are aware of how what they say can be used out of context, and that a pre-recorded interview can be cut to show a subject in a good or bad light. Remember that how you start the interview sets the tone for the exchange: make sure you get the person's name and any other vital details correct!

Interviewees tend to fall into three main categories:

- the general public – achievers, victims, observers, those with specialist interests, those with a reaction or an opinion
- corporate representatives, spokesmen and women, politicians, experts
- celebrities – stars and renowned artists from all areas of the media, models, sportsmen and women and infamous characters who have made it into the newspapers.

Most guests will either want to promote something, or wish to express an opinion. The TV interview offers them just this opportunity, in exchange for answering a few questions. In some cases they will have their own agenda and try to dictate how the interview should run. Hard-nosed business representatives and politicians often request a list of questions. Only in extremely rare circumstances should you consent, although you may wish to outline the interview by telling them how long it will last and giving them an idea of the sort of questions you will be asking. It remains a sensitive area as to how much you brief your guest. In essence this applies to all forms of interviewing, since you want the reaction to your questions to be fresh and instinctive, not considered and then countered with a bland answer.

'They like to ask how you are going to start. If this means giving them an advantage – if I've got some "killer blow" – I don't say, or I'll say that I'm not quite sure yet. On the whole I'm very reluctant to be seen giving away an advantage. Professional politicians should be able to handle anything.'
Huw Edwards (BBC 6 O'Clock News, formerly political correspondent at Westminster)

INTERVIEW 'PROTOCOL'

It's always courteous to introduce yourself to your guest before the programme if circumstances allow. A brief chat might reveal some new, more relevant and up-to-the-moment information that you didn't have earlier. It also shows a willingness to help them feel at ease in what will be, for many, an unfamiliar and potentially hostile environment. Members of the general public who have a story to tell need reassurance that they are in safe hands with you. The element of trust is all-important.

Whoever you are interviewing, establish – prior to going on air – how your guest would like to be addressed. Christina? Chris? Tina? Ms West? Professor? Your Honour? Being corrected on air weakens your position. Do not be dominated by an overpowering guest: be patient and keep cool, calm and collected. Remember that you may want to interview them again at a later date, so always be polite. Be sensitive, too, to any subject that the guest does not want to talk about. On one occasion, a TV actress was invited on to a morning chat show, having first made it clear that she was not prepared to discuss a particular TV role she had played. She said that if she was asked about it, she would walk out. The presenter hadn't read the researcher's notes and began the interview on that very subject. Shocked by such a blatant disregard of her wishes, she sat in silence until the co-presenter was able to coax her into talking about something else. This was a very frosty and uncomfortable interview from which no one, including the viewer, benefited.

TYPES OF INTERVIEW

There are as many different types of interview as there are topics to discuss, and each requires a different strategy. Current affairs programmes and light entertainment necessitate different rules of engagement. Essentially, there are two approaches to interviewing:

- *Confrontational.* Asking hard, exacting questions which require direct answers. Hard news (headline current affairs) demands a more incisive approach. With journalistic background, the interviewer will search out facts and debate reasoned arguments. They will challenge and pursue a determined line of questioning until a straightforward answer is given.
- *Supportive and encouraging.* The interviewer will elicit information in a calm and friendly manner. Soft news (soft feature news items) and light entertainment favour a more conversational style, less pressurised for the guest. That isn't to say that the topics covered carry no weight, but the emphasis is generally more on personal experience and amusement.

Celebrity interviews

It is intimidating to meet your own personal hero. Everybody has one: a movie star, an astronaut, a financial wizard, an explorer, a tennis player. There is no preparation for this first meeting. No matter how cool you tell yourself to be, the flutter of excitement will rise up in you. It's quite natural to get tongue-tied – but you have to find a way to overcome your awe and admiration and get on with your question.

The showbiz celebrity interview can present you with a whole cluster of unique problems: Michael Parkinson fighting off Rod Hull's Emu puppet comes to mind; and an intoxicated Oliver Reed, staggering to his seat and trying to engage in conversation with Michael Aspel, remains legendary. Some great movie stars have been struck dumb, unable to speak at all, while others give a brief answer or resort to an anecdote. All are wary of being asked too personal a question. The megastars have publicists who lay down strict conditions on what can and cannot be asked, and it is becoming increasingly harder to touch on any subject remotely personal. Nevertheless, a well-structured question can slip under their guard and produce an interesting reply.

Junket interviews

Whether due to demand, a desire for security or maybe even hype, many film and music stars have taken to doing 'conveyor belt' interviews. A stream of journalists and reporters are invited to attend, ushered in one by one and given 15 or 20 minutes. Time is strictly limited and interviews monitored. Showbiz reporter Matt Cain says, 'It's always a challenge to find or phrase questions in a way that hasn't been done 15 times already that morning. The star will end up giving pat answers. Equally important is to set up an immediate rapport – an interview can live or die from that.'

Children

This is a section of society that is notoriously hard to interview. That bright little six-year-old who won't stop chattering during rehearsal suddenly loses the power of speech and barely nods in recognition of anything you say. Be prepared and ready to prompt. Never ask kids 'yes' or 'no' questions; always use 'open' ones – who, what, why, when, how.

Just as difficult is the child who is easily distracted. The camera and the lighting, even your shoelaces can unleash a torrent of comments and questions which, to them, are far more interesting than anything you had planned. Improvise and pray that this will be over soon!

GETTING THE INTERVIEW

Capturing your guest can take patience and diplomacy. Most prospective guests are only too willing to take up the opportunity of a TV interview, but some may play hard to get for personal reasons. Michael Parkinson reportedly took Peter Sellers out for lunch five times before he would agree to appear on his show. Whoever it is you wish to question, approach with courtesy and professionalism. A major hurdle is to get past the personal assistants and publicists who can act as an impenetrable shield: try to have patience and gain their trust. Once you are in conversation with the PR contact they may succumb to your charms and do everything they can to help you. They may even unknowingly offer an illuminating insight into your subject. Friends can also set up introductions to their own friends and colleagues. Network! Attend parties! If you are fortunate enough, your programme may have a researcher to do the 'leg work' for you. In their pursuit of a subject they may have learnt a valuable fact or two. Listen to their suggestions.

BE WELL BRIEFED

A major prerequisite for a successful interview is research. You can't have enough of it; it provides the fuel for your questions and gives you confidence. In the event of a guest 'clamming up' or refusing to answer questions, you will have enough resources to get out of trouble and rescue the situation if you are well briefed. Having information shows respect for your guest and even flatters them with the knowledge that you've done your homework. With that reassurance they may feel more inclined to open up, offering revelations that no one has heard before.

Use every avenue open to you:

- read current articles and refer to other experts in that field
- check your facts and make sure that all your information is up to date
- take a look at all the relevant VTs being used in the interview – is there anything you can use that will lead you to your next question?
- always pick the brains of the researchers and read their notes
- during the interview, listen out for the editor on talkback, who may have an interesting question for you to ask. It's hard to listen to talkback and the interviewee at the same time, but you do need to be alert to both.

On your list of questions you might consider adding the name(s) of your guest(s) and specific place names you want to include. It's frightening how in the heat of the interview these very important titles slip out of the brain. And finally, practise hard-to-pronounce words out loud.

LISTEN TO THE ANSWERS

This may seem obvious, but you do need to listen carefully and respond appropriately to the answer just given. It may be that your guest has just offered a new piece of information that is worth pursuing. If you are flexible and open-minded, you won't miss this opportunity to develop the interview.

THE TIME FACTOR

A dominant factor in your interview is the amount of time that you are allocated. This can be dictated by the programme producer or by the interviewee themselves. Choose the most important questions and aim to cover all the relevant information in the time allowed. It's better to have more questions than time permits – in case the interviewee needs prompting or you are offered more time – than to be left making it up or looking blank. Listen to the director in your earpiece and/or keep an eye out for the floor manager who may be instructing you to lengthen or shorten the interview.

Timing your last question can be the hardest part of the job. Prepare yourself and the guest for the end of the interview: 'And briefly . . .' Decide *before* you start, how you will finish. What will be your 'out cue'? At 15 seconds you have to wind up the interview and at 5 seconds you are saying thank-you. Most interviewers thank their interviewees before they move on. It's polite, and signals to everyone – viewer, interviewee and production gallery – that you've finished.

TIPS FOR EFFECTIVE INTERVIEWING

- KISS (Keep It Short and Simple). Ask one question at a time.
- Use quotes. These are very difficult to wriggle out of: 'You are reported in the *Evening Albatross* as saying that . . .'
- Avoid butting in with another question. Interrupt only when necessary. If the subject is not answering your question, find a natural pause or intake of breath to speak up on the viewers' behalf. As well as being irritating, interjections make cutting the interview later in the editing suite much more difficult.
- Don't finish their sentences for them. It's annoying, and as you are not telepathic you can't be certain that's how the sentence would have finished. However, you may have to help out if they've gone blank.
- Avoid repeating the answer you've just been given – for example, 'I had my suspicions.' 'You had your suspicions?' On TV, this is just a waste of time.
- Allow pauses. Presenters are quite naturally reluctant to allow time for a pause, having a sense that something should be happening all the time. It's fine to allow the interviewee a moment for thought but it must be an active pause, with 'something' going on. Stay in the moment, listening keenly. Nodding in agreement, a smile, a tilt of the head or mirroring the interviewee's posture are all effective. If the interview isn't a live broadcast, most of these pauses can be edited out later as they will have served their purpose.
- Judge your persistence. Know when enough is enough. Don't be too strident and/or too pushy. If you attack unnecessarily the viewer will see you as a bully. The exception is hard news or when you're faced with an evasive reply and you know the viewer wants an answer. In such situations you have to be sure of your facts and the reason for which you are pursuing that question.

- Use your voice carefully. It's not always simply a matter of structuring the question appropriately, you need to use a suitable tone of voice too. Resist the natural tendency to raise your voice as the temperature of the interview hots up. The exception to this is when you are purposefully provoking a reaction. It's a technical trick to employ whilst you remain internally cool.
- Speak clearly and keep the energy in your voice. It wastes valuable time if the presenter has to be asked to repeat themselves.
- Remember that not all interviewees will be in the studio. If you are interviewing via a monitor, be prepared for a small delay. This is more common when a satellite link is used to another country. Keep your vocal volume up and speak clearly. They can usually only hear you via an earpiece, so remember that the interviewee can't see your face even though they seem to be talking straight at you. They will be talking direct to a camera lens and may not have a monitor feeding back your image.
- Try to remain neutral. Don't let your own opinions and views colour your questioning. The viewer wants to know what your guest thinks.

'It's very dangerous to get caught up in the emotion of a story. You'll always be remembered for that outburst and may feel very silly two years down the line. Emotional engagement opens you up to the charge that you didn't see the whole picture. If you become emotionally involved in one side of a story, you can't really offer anything independent or impartial.'
Jeremy Vine (BBC Newsnight)

BODY LANGUAGE

In Chapter 3, I stressed the importance of body language, and here again I emphasise the value of remaining physically engaged and attentive. You may hear the term 'let the camera in': that's a warning that you are physically excluding the viewer. Try to keep the angle open so that your arm and shoulder do not create a barrier between yourself and the viewer. When holding a microphone between yourself and an interviewee, hold it in the hand away from the camera, not across your body. For your own benefit, and purely technically, try to avoid sharp and unflattering profiles. The following are some more guidelines on body language when interviewing.

- If the interviewee is not in the studio but on a live link and can be seen on a screen or monitor, then turn to talk directly to their image.

- In the case of viewer phone-ins, where you can't see the caller, look straight at the camera lens. Listen and talk directly to them. In a memorable phone-in to a US chat show, the presenter and her guests all looked up at the ceiling and talked to the loudspeakers where the voice was coming from. It looked very silly!
- If you are conducting an interview with a fixed single camera – whether in the studio or on location (in the field, on the road) – then the interviewee will be shot from only one angle, generally over your shoulder. Once the interviewee has left, the camera will be repositioned to focus on you, at which point you will then be filmed repeating your questions, nodding sagely and responding accordingly. Try to remember how you originally responded to the different answers. On occasion a co-operative interviewee will stay to help give you an eyeline and fill out the picture, but if you are on your own it will require some acting. These reaction shots are known as 'noddies' or 'reverses'.
- Choose appropriate clothing to maintain a balance between style of programme and topic (*see* also Chapter 3, pp. 24–33).

YOU AND YOUR ENVIRONMENT

Interviews can take place anywhere. The presenter must deal with all the conditions and eventualities that outside broadcasting can produce.

In the open

There are some physical aspects to look out for when interviewing outside. Look carefully at how you are framed. The camera operator should be helping you, but don't rely 100% on that – work together. Ask nicely to have a look through the viewfinder to see for yourself. Take some responsibility and suggest a relevant background, keeping an eye open for distracting signs and hoardings.

Distracting action can also be your enemy. If your item includes that car swinging from a crane, then it should be in the background. If it doesn't, move away. However, there's no way you can be sure that a 'lurker' won't appear behind you waving a 'Hello Mum' sign to the camera. If it's a recorded piece to camera you'll just need the patience to go again. Some extraneous noises can be filtered out technically and may only be distracting to you. Concentrate.

Most presenters agree that reporting 'in the field' is less pressurised than working from the studio. There are fewer technical restraints and your focus is on one item rather than holding the show together, unless of course your whole show is filmed outside. Physically – because the camera shot is generally wider, allowing space for scenery around you – there is more freedom to move and make bigger, more relaxed, less restrained gestures. It's wise to make a reconnaissance of any paths you intend to walk down, though: look out for holes, steps, wobbly paving stones, low beams and branches. The natural elements will also contrive to feature in your report. The viewer expects a certain amount of live natural action, so without being totally distracted, it's fine to react to your environment and, if it's relevant, mention it:

> 'You join us here on Southport Sands for the building of the world's biggest sandcastle. Despite this heavy downpour work continues, and in some cases radical repairs to the rain-drenched ramparts. It's an heroic effort.'

> 'As you can hear the crowd are really enjoying themselves. In fact their singing is so loud I can hardly hear myself talking.'

INTERVIEWING MORE THAN ONE PERSON AT A TIME

In such situations your role expands to that of a discussion facilitator, and demands that you listen even more intently. Keep the interviewees to the point. Certainly, curb the conversation-hoggers and make sure that everyone has a say. Try to keep a balance. Where an audience is actively involved in the studio, your task as arbiter is even more important. Chat shows can become emotional and vociferous when the audience gets personally involved or guests react unexpectedly or irrationally. It's considered great TV, but the presenter needs to exert strong authority and influence over the proceedings whilst still maintaining a relationship with the viewer.

When addressing a guest, name them. That way, no one gets confused about who you're talking to. It focuses attention on that one guest, and technically it alerts the director to the person who is going to speak next so they can cut to a close-up of them. Have separate questions ready for each guest.

If you follow a few simple rules, things should go smoothly:

- clarify questions where necessary
- reprimand question 'side steppers'
- contain outbursts of emotion
- keep a balanced argument
- keep to time.

TYPES OF QUESTION

There are many different forms of questions, but to get the information you want, you need to phrase them effectively. What do you want to know? Bear in mind that this may change with the response, and therefore it's important to remain focused but flexible.

Open and closed questions

Questions fall predominantly into these two categories. Open questions encourage the subject to answer with more than a one-word reply or a blunt yes or no. Such a response can be a presenter's nightmare. Open questions invite the interviewee to reveal more information and spark free and liberated discussion. Closed questions – such as 'How many?', 'What is the name of . . .?' – ask for a direct and specific answer. They restrict the reply, and can be useful if the interviewee is being evasive to open questions. Both forms of questioning can be very effective when used appropriately.

Open comparative questions
These are really useful questions, as they allow the interviewee to respond with an opinion based on experience and to answer in some detail: 'What differences have you noticed over the past twelve months?'

Opinion-seeking questions
These give the interviewee an opportunity to express themselves in more depth: 'What do you feel about that?' 'In your opinion, what qualities would a dog-walker need?'

Leading questions
These assume a particular reply, and suggest that there is only one desired answer. The guest will either confirm your view, in which case the next question will be an open question such as 'Why?', or they will have to correct your statement before replying with their own thoughts: 'Why is it that people say fox-hunting is an inhumane act?' 'I take it that you believe . . .'

Empathising questions
This form of questioning indicates that you are able to understand an emotional response – or that you are trying to interpret it. It gives you an opportunity to explore more closely the interviewee's feelings and beliefs: 'I see, so in the light of that how does it feel to be so let down?'

Emotional questions
An emotional plea can often unsettle your guest and force them to answer a question in a way that they hadn't intended: 'Can you honestly say that . . .?' 'Don't you have any feelings for their plight?'

Clarifying questions
By listening carefully you may notice some discrepancies in people's responses to your questions. Clarifying questions require more explanation, more details and fuller answers: 'What do you mean by that?' 'What other choices are there?'

Hypothetical questions
This style is often rebuffed as being merely speculative. You really need time and the trust of your interviewee to pursue this line of questioning: 'Just suppose that you had unlimited resources . . .'

Summarising questions
These are generally concerned with interpreting answers and confirming facts and opinions: 'As I understand it . . .' 'Are you saying that . . .?' They are also useful for bringing a discussion or interview to a close, and drawing attention to the salient points: 'It's clear that you've had some severe ups and downs and yet managed to come through smiling. Good luck with the festival and thank you for coming in.'

IN SUMMARY

When interviewing, remember the following key guidelines.

- Make sure that all your information is up to date. Check your facts.
- Research – consult PR, newsclippings and experts in the relevant field.
- Make sure that you have been fully and accurately briefed.
- Check all relevant VTs and use them to link back into the interview.
- Have clear questions, and in some cases, a very clear idea of the answers that you're after.
- What are the key points? Write out key questions on cue cards and any quotes you wish to refer to.
- Write down the name(s) of the interviewee(s) and relevant place names.
- Check how the interviewees would like to be addressed, and respect their wishes.
- Check your environment – set and scenery, location backdrops and

walkways.
- Establish a rapport on initial contact.
- Take control.
- Keep your questions within the timeframe.
- Listen to talkback.
- Speak clearly.
- Actively listen. Think about your body language.
- Step back from confrontation. Detach your emotions.
- Aim to be conversational, with a genuine interest in the subject; and directed, with a genuine interest in the information.

EXERCISES
Practice is vital. Talk to people and widen your knowledge. Get into the habit of asking questions. Interviewing friends and family is an excellent place to start: try local shopkeepers, friends and neighbours. Don't use a video camera at first – the following exercises are for you to practise questioning and listening. If you wish, use a small audio recording equipment and review your efforts later. Once you feel comfortable interviewing you can then ask a friend to film you as you repeat any of the exercises.

(1)   *Vocation or pastime* – interview someone who owns an allotment. Ask them how they started. How often they tend their patch. What do they grow? What are the benefits? Find an angle to pursue, an 'agenda': for example, growing your own vegetables; threat from developers.

(2)   *Action* – interview someone with a car. Ask them to talk you through changing a tyre.

(3)   *Experience* – ask someone about their holiday. Remember to find an angle and keep to the point.

(4)   *Insight* – approach a local amateur dramatic society. Interview the leading actor or director for their thoughts on the play.

(5)   *Review* – this is excellent practice for reporting. All presenters are likely to be asked to review or give their opinion on any given event, sport, wine, theatre, musical event, holiday resort, local fair, business takeover, departmental expansion. You name it, whatever it is there's always someone with an opinion about it. Research one of the above, and present the piece to camera.

(6)   Think of three famous people you would like to interview. Give yourself a reason why. List at least two facts about

them. What questions would you like to ask them? Prepare an interview as if you had 5 minutes with each one.

(7) Be interviewed yourself on any given topic. Understand what it feels like.

WHAT THEY SAY

'Ask yourself, what do I actually want to get out of this person? If I were sitting at home, what would I want to know? And keep on asking them a range of questions until you get the answer or the information you are looking for.'
Kirsty Lang (Channel 4 News)

'It's no good talking about things you have no knowledge of. The audience wants to believe you, and to feel that you have a good grasp of the facts.'
Jon Snow (Channel 4 News)

'I'm 100% red hot on research. Often, you are given a researcher. Talk to them, they are invaluable. It's good manners to ask your guest intelligent questions – it breeds respect and confidence. You look like a dingbat if you don't know what you're talking about!'
Julie Peasgood (BBC Pebble Mill, Children in Need)

'I see myself as representing the viewer. If there's an obvious question, then ask it. The job is to understand the subject yourself and to work out a way to explain it to others. You are expected to be on top of what's in the papers or on the radio. I always allow myself two hours just for research, but it's never enough.'
Simon McCoy (SKY News)

16

Chroma Key
and Virtual Studio

Presenters should have a basic understanding of both these technical imaging functions so that they can present with ease – even though the set or image to which they are referring is not real, but computer-generated.

CHROMA KEY

This device is most commonly seen in weather forecast bulletins, but can also be used in different kinds of programme. In news or current affairs, a chroma-key 'window' may appear in the corner of the screen upon which is a graphic – a still or moving picture. If the presenter were to look up over their shoulder, they would not see the image; it's only visible to the viewer (although if the presenter has an output monitor they will see the whole picture as the viewer does). For instance, the weather presenter appears to be standing in front of a weather map displaying information that changes with the report. In reality, the presenter is standing in front of a taut cloth or scenic flat that has been painted chroma key blue or green. The map and all the visual information is electronically stored and mixed with the 'reality picture' (the presenter) in the gallery.

At the press of a button the electronic image can change. Blue, brilliant green and bright yellow are the most favoured colours for chroma-key background, as they are most distant from skin tone. The chroma key process recognises the chosen colour and removes it from the picture, replacing it with the map and any related information. It will also recognise the chosen colour from anywhere else in the picture and that includes clothing – so that if the presenter wears blue, the clothing will appear transparent, revealing the computer-generated image. However, most equipment used today is sensitive enough to detect shades of colour, so that you may be able to get away with wearing a very dark or very pale shade of blue without the risk of appearing to have a hole straight through you. Be advised by the director.

The other main concern for the presenter working with chroma key is having sufficient and accurate knowledge of what is appearing in the chroma-key window. It's essential to rehearse thoroughly and use an output monitor on the studio floor. You may need to facially or verbally acknowledge what you cannot see but wish to refer to. Alternatively, as in the case of the weather presenter, actually point to details and specific areas. An incorrect response to the changing graphics and pictures will undermine your credibility. The presenter, then, must stay close to the chroma-key window whilst it is being used, in order to stay in shot. The background image is created in the gallery and will not respond to any camera movement. If the camera pans to left or right, the background will remain static and part of the image will be lost in the frame – a most unnatural effect.

VIRTUAL STUDIO

The limitations of chroma key are overcome in the virtual studio. In most cases a small box with sensors is fixed to the top of the camera. Electronically linked to the computer, it translates all that is seen into data which drives the computer and renders the virtual set into real time. A 3D model can be created in the computer, so that as the camera moves, so does the virtual world. The sensors detect movement and allow the presenter to run around the set, or jump and climb stairs, as the computer-generated images will keep in step. The camera can tilt, pan, zoom and track from side to side and the computer will respond immediately. It can even tilt up to the studio lights or go beyond the edges of a real set, enabling the presenter to make a complete circle in a virtual world. As the camera pans to the edge of the set the computer switches to a 'garbage mat' that has been programmed with designed virtual images. For instance, a presenter in a virtual jungle looks upwards and the camera tilts to follow their eye. In reality, the shot would be of studio lighting; in a virtual studio the viewer sees the roof of the jungle.

For programme-makers, the advantages of virtual studio are enormous. First of all, it's cost-effective. A conventional studio has to be constructed and later transported and stored. With virtual studio (or virtual reality – VR, as it's sometimes called) a whole set can be designed with videos and photos stored on disk and used again and again. A presenter can be seen walking along a virtual Caribbean beach without the expense of filming on location. A spacious corporate office can be designed using the same studio. In fact, many believe that in the future there will be scope for broadcasting a series of programmes one after the other using completely different virtual sets. For instance, after a half-hour financial programme in a virtual studio, a new package could be loaded into the computer during the commercial break. This would take only a few minutes. Then, with a change of chair and two new presenters, a programme on pottery could be broadcast on a different virtual set. Imaginative designers can make each set as stylised and outrageous as they wish. Producers agree that it would be financially and physically impossible to achieve the many illusions they can create in a small studio space that they can in a virtual studio.

The second major advantage of virtual studio is that it opens up a whole world of creative and imaginative opportunities, particularly useful in education. A journey through time can be created in moments, linking quickly from set to set. Switching from a mediaeval market place to a futuristic trading hall and back to a Roman forum in a matter of seconds becomes a possibility. The virtual studio is a concept already being used extensively in US TV and in mainland Europe. Game shows are already experimenting with it and producing some wild effects. It's easy to see that in science fiction and historical movies, the technology has already been embraced.

How does virtual studio affect the TV presenter?
As with chroma key, the clothing colour issue remains the same. A virtual studio, including the floor, is painted chroma-key blue or green. Choose colours and shades of clothing that will not be selected by the computer and be advised by the director.

In a virtual studio, the presenter has to become something of an actor, reacting to objects and effects that they cannot see. It can be quite a liberating experience with no props or furniture to inhibit your performance, but at the same time you need to be aware of the imagined world. It is essential to know the geography of the set. Whilst strategically placed monitors can assist, you do not want to be constantly referring to them. Technology can help you to interact with the virtual world by removing the words from the prompter screen on the camera and replacing them with the picture of the studio output. This gives you the chance to talk to the viewer and at the same time see what is going on in the virtual set. Remember that what you see on the output monitor is a reverse shot. If you move to the left it will appear on the screen as if you've moved to the right. To help presenters, reverse scan monitors are often used. This gives a mirror image, which is far easier for the presenter to work with. An alternative idea is to paint an output monitor surround chroma-key blue and select tones of blue on the screen. It's then possible to put it on the set and use it as a reference without being picked up and seen by the sensors. Another trick to aid your memory is to write crib notes on the set with the same chroma-key colour marker pen. Don't even think about doing this without checking with the floor manager first!

Computer-generated static objects are easier to navigate if they can be marked out with blue tape on the studio floor. All your eyelines need to be rehearsed if there is no fixed object to relate to. Here are a few examples you may encounter.

- A presenter refers to a picture which appears to one side of them and they are instructed to walk towards it. Mark a spot on the floor where you need to stop. Be guided by the director where to look and fix that spot in your mind.
- Climbing stairs or stepping on and off a rostrum need not be a problem. Generally a chroma-key painted step will be put on the correct marks so that you physically make the move.
- The same principle applies to desks, chairs and sofas. It's possible to sit, perch or lie on the chroma-key painted furniture and let the virtual reality designer create the set. You can still put papers and props on the desk but you cannot leave them there, for when the image changes they will be left suspended in mid-air. A real chair painted blue provides the presenter with somewhere to sit whilst the computer generates a more design-conscious seat. Without moving, the presenter can one moment be sitting in the studio on a leather chair, and the next on a wooden stool. A more adventurous designer may have you sitting on a train seat, then on a park bench and next on the steps of an Italian cathedral. In response, you should physically change your posture to relate realistically to your different virtual surroundings.
- Larger pieces of furniture such as a column need a little bit more attention. The base of the column can be marked out on the studio floor, but as with the window effect, you will need to adjust your eyeline to indicate size and height.
- Anything you have to move, touch or open will require more of your acting skills as you have to visualise the set and effects. It's a good idea to practise with a similar object and then remember how it feels. However, wrestling with an imagined 25-legged sea monster, or dancing with a 6-foot gerbil, can really test your talents!

When it goes wrong

Currently, virtual reality is rarely used in live situations, so you should have plenty of opportunity to rehearse and re-record. According to producers, there is usually enough technical back-up to cover most eventualities. Re-booting the whole system only takes a couple of seconds and they can very quickly go to a commercial break or run a VT. But as in all emergency events, the presenter has to think on their feet and cover as best they can with appropriate ad libbing.

EXERCISES

(1) Open and close a real door. Notice the shape of the handle. What did it feel like? How did it operate? Stand away from it and mime doing it just as you did it for real.

(2) Lean on a real fence or waist-high wall. Take note of your posture and where your hands and arms rest. Step back a couple of metres away from the structure and recreate the position. Go back to the real structure and judge for yourself how well you did.

(3) Gather a selection of objects and examine each one. Consider the difference in weight, size and texture. You will notice that you pick up and handle each one differently. When you feel familiar with them, push them to one side and mime picking them up and putting them down. Try to recreate your physical response to each.

(4) Gather a selection of bigger objects and do the same. Miming accurately is not enough – you will need to show your reaction with your whole body.

IN SUMMARY

- Pay attention to the colour and shade you are wearing. Bring alternative clothing.
- Learn to work in an imagined world, increasing your mime skills.
- Know the geography of the set and ensure that important images are laid out with markers.
- Make sure you can see the preview monitors.

WHAT THEY SAY

'It's a huge playground, but rehearsal is most important. Being able to see the monitors and having vital communication via the earpiece is invaluable. I always ask the producer or director to give me an audio prompt as to where we're going next. Rehearse segments and then transmit it. Know the virtual set, otherwise you'll be falling off cliffs or bumping into walls.

You have to be more accurate in what you do than in conventional studios. One error, for instance, is sitting in a seat that's in the real world but not present in the virtual world. The viewer will be on the lookout for more mistakes and not interested in what you are saying. The whole point of using virtual will have been for nothing.

Technology should aid the subject you are talking about. It's a question for debate whether in the future, producers will mention whether a report is coming from a virtual studio or a real location. Reporters could put on a duffel coat and pretend they are in Kosovo, with a wind machine for effect. Not ethical, but who knows.'
Martin Stanford (producer and presenter SKY TV)

'As long as it helps people understand something more clearly then it achieves its purpose. But there's a risk that it can become a bit gimmicky – effects for effects' sake. It does bring out the actor in you.'
Simon McCoy (SKY News)

'Some devices are useful but only to illustrate a point. What you see in our studio is what you get – it's honest.'
Jon Snow (Channel 4 News)

'It can be a bit of a guessing game. Rehearsing is really important, and listening to the director through talkback. They'll guide you and give you the right eyeline. And they can edit the best pieces together later.'
Kirsten O'Brien (BBC Youth Programmes)

Part Three

THE VERSATILE
PRESENTER

17

The Continuity Announcer

The continuity announcer is also known as the 'anchor', the 'link', or just simply the 'announcer'. The job involves exactly that – announcing and introducing the next programme or schedule of programmes for the day. But it's more than that, and more than just having a pleasant voice – although that's important too. The announcer's principal task is to keep the viewer with the channel. At the end of a programme, viewers tend to flick through channels to see what else is on, or get up and do something else. For that reason TV executives will focus a lot of attention on these 'junctions' (connecting links between programmes) in an attempt to hold the viewers. Many of the larger TV stations and networks will have whole departments dedicated to their presentation.

The announcer is seen as the host of the TV station, inviting the audience to watch the forthcoming programmes. They are chosen for their ability to reflect the style of the station, the segment of programmes they will introduce and the audience the TV station aims to attract. A mature, resonant, intellectual style of presentation would not suit a target audience of 5 to 8 year olds and, equally, the youthful, effervescent qualities of children's presentation may be deemed unsuitable for a political debate and documentary segment. Styles vary, but the essential remit of the job remains the same: hold the viewer to the channel.

Working as the viewer's programme guide, it's important that you know what you are promoting, who is in it and if any parental guidance is needed. Research plays an important role in this job. As announcer, you are also the voice of the station when technical hiccups occur. The viewer wants to know that everything is under control and that they'll be able to watch the programme they had planned to see – or if not, why not. They want to know why there is a break in vision or a change of scheduled programmes, or why programmes are running late. Remain relaxed and maintain audience confidence. When chaos and panic is breaking out in all the technical departments, it is your task to keep calm and display great control.

There are predominantly two forms of programme-announcing. The *station announcer* generally uses the more traditional linking and introduction format, providing a regular input of practical and concise information. Within that framework there is still scope to add humour and wit and references to the viewer's previous knowledge of the programme, so the content does not necessarily have to be dry. More often than not, a station announcer is out of vision, so excellent vocal skills are required. The task is to vocally entice and intrigue the viewer as well as deliver plain, direct facts: 'Now on Trunk TV, *The News.*' It's a fine balance between persuasive friend and enthusiastic role-player, but remember that you are introducing a programme and not demonstrating your brilliant acting talent. Colour descriptive words without being too lyrical, and without over-selling the forthcoming programme. Keep a brightness and energy in your voice. That's easier said than done; you are likely to spend long, dreary hours in a small, stuffy, soundproofed booth. Unfortunately, this is not a guaranteed route to an 'on screen' career, but it does provide you with an excellent foundation in the workings of TV programming and the demands of presentation. It also pays very well. Add to that having regular shifts, planned well in advance so you can organise the rest of your life, and you're looking at an attractive job.

Segment linking within an overall programme is more common in youth-dedicated slots, e.g. CBBC or Channel 5 on a Saturday morning. Here the presenters link a variety of programmes with the extra demand of establishing a proactive rapport with their audience. Between the cartoons and mini-dramas, personal birthday messages are read out, live interviews take place and games and competitions keep the viewer tuned in. These linking segments become as important as the programme the presenter is there to introduce – and sometimes they become programmes in their own right.

SOME PRACTICAL GUIDELINES FOR ANNOUNCING

The continuity announcer is the constant voice to which the viewer returns after each programme. You become the anchor – hence the name – and a familiar presence. Whether in vision or not your personality can come through. Out of vision you need to work your voice harder to highlight important details and mood. Here are some practical guidelines for announcing:

- Relax.
- Start on the voice, the first word. You don't have time to warm into it.
- You are the host to a wide variety of people, but you still need to use the technique of talking to only one friend. This applies equally to in-vision and voice-over.
- Vocally 'point out' the programme name and time of transmission. Give extra emphasis to this if it differs from what has been advertised.
- Have a clear image of the programme that you're talking about. Visualise it.
- Think through what you're saying.
- Give yourself time. Don't race the text. Whilst it's imperative that you have plenty to talk about (you can always extend or trim as time demands), you'll need to mentally recognise 5, 10 or 15 seconds and be able to fit your chat into that time without being cut off mid-sentence. Remember that on average we speak at 3 words per second. If you have a script before going on air, time it. If it's an unscripted section but your chat has to fit into a time limit, rehearse aloud and time it.
- If you are using a slide or any other visual, make sure that your words fit the action and any named persons.
- At every junction adopt the mood and tone of your presentation to suit the programme. Take care not to overact. A mere indication of mood will suffice.
- Annunciate clearly and keep your voice alert, especially at the end of the sentence.

SCRIPTING

Most TV presentation departments have teams of directors creating programme trailers which, as a continuity announcer, you will be invited to 'voice'. In other words, you'll be asked to read their scripts. For major new dramas and specific comedy shows, the original production company may provide their own trailers which are bought in as a package.

The TV announcer/presenter generally writes the link scripts. These are short programme promotions, the content of which is variable and dependent on when it will be announced. This could be within a run-down of the day's schedule, during the credits of the previous programme, before a commercial break or directly before the pro-gramme itself. Although it's usual to write your own scripts it can happen that someone else has written them for you. The benefit is that half your job is done; the downside is that you have got to make someone else's words and style work for you and make them sound as if they are your own.

Scripting requires some skill, summarising in 10, 30 or 50 words the plot of a film or the gist of a gardening programme, or finding a reason to watch wildlife in the Antarctic or a financial debate with the heads of African mineral companies. It also necessitates long hours of viewing programmes you wouldn't watch if you had any choice in the matter and then writing persuasively about them. If you want to ensure that your script is accurate, it's your duty to watch – even in fast forward. TV network scripts will usually be checked and edited, and sometimes rewritten, by the network director or presentation director. Ultimately they have the final word on what is transmitted. Be prepared to accept their criticism.

SEGMENTS IN A PROGRAMME SCHEDULE

The segments allocated for continuity announcing are named in a programme schedule. They are as follows:

The menu
This is the inclusion of the programme within part or a whole list of the day's viewing. There may be six or seven items on the list, so to avoid an information overload each one will need to be very brief and punchy. 'Time for another shopping spree with Jackie Lane at 8.30. and at 9, our blockbuster movie is the breathtaking *Titanic*.'

The holder
This announcement for the next programme is made immediately after one programme has finished or as the credits are rolling. Appropriately called a 'holder', its duration is generally 10, 12 or 15 seconds and its aim is to hold the audience's attention over the commercial break or

news bulletin. It's there to tempt the viewer into staying with your channel.

'Love and passion on a massive scale next tonight, as we board *Titanic* and embark on the legendary liner's catastrophic voyage. With startling special effects, James Cameron's award-winning film stars Kate Winslet and Leonardo Di Caprio. That's in just a few minutes.' (15 seconds duration)

The introduction

A short line of script spoken directly before the programme. The visual used in this slot is usually a still or an animated logo of the station ident. As well as introducing the programme, the announcer also identifies and markets the station. There's no need to be verbally fancy here – the viewer is already seated, so announce clearly and in a manner appropriate to the programme . . . and the TV station.

'Now on CHANNEL 224, hang on to your lifebelts as we set sail, aboard . . . *Titanic.*'

A word of warning – note how the programme starts. As with any link, don't repeat what's said at the beginning of the programme. It's boring and shows a total lack of imagination. For instance, you want to avoid your script reading, 'Now on The Cookery Channel, Adele is cooking up something special,' if the programme begins with: 'Hello I'm Adele. I'm cooking something special.'

Back anno and pointers

An announcer may also be required to write a back announcement. This is a tag to a programme giving extra information. For example: change of transmission time, follow-up programmes, available brochures and books.

'The book accompanying this series, *Adele's Fayre*, is available at most bookshops, priced £9.99. Next week Adele cooks up a traditional English breakfast without grease, at the later time of 9.30.'

The end of the programme is also an opportunity to point out related programmes. The connection can be theme-related, such as other cookery programmes, or it may a more tenuous link – such as the actors or presenters appearing in another programme, or the same location being used.

TECHNICAL PROBLEMS

(*See* also Chapter 14 on Breakdowns.) The good news here is that many TV stations use pre-recorded announcements. However, if the continuity is 'live' then you should always have a backup script at the ready or a copy of the programme schedule. Find out what the problems are so that you can, in a calm and relaxed manner, reassure the viewer that their favourite programme will be back very shortly. Remember you are the host. We're in your hands and we could so easily change stations. Keep cool, calm and collected.

EXERCISES
(1)   Take a look at a film guide. Pick one that you know and see how different writers have summarised it or have written a trailer for it. Then have a go yourself.
(2)   Choose a 3-hour timeframe from a TV guide and write a 30-second menu which will include at least four different programmes.
(3)   From that menu select one programme and write a holder for it (*see* above). Allow 15 seconds. Read it aloud and time it. Make an audio recording and judge for yourself whether you would be tempted to watch.
(4)   Using the same chosen programme, write a 5-second introduction.

18

The Voice-Over

A voice-over can be simply described as out-of-vision speech or spoken commentary. It requires huge amounts of concentration and an ability to convey attitudes and emotions in a single spoken word. In effect, to vocally bring to life the written text.

As a TV presenter, you will be expected to be able to voice-over anything and everything – and because of your on-screen talents all sorts of voice-over work will come your way. The term 'voice-over' describes both the job and the person who performs it. The performer is also commonly called 'the voice-over artist', 'the voice', 'MVO' or 'FVO'; and the script is referred to as 'the copy'.

The voice-over can be required for numerous projects and they mainly fall into the following categories.

- TV, film and radio promotions – continuity announcing and programme trailers
- TV and radio commercials
- a report – voicing-over an item of news (delivered by the reporter or TV journalist, not a voice-over artist)
- narration and documentaries – voicing-over a filmed sequence
- corporate or promotional videos – promoting products and companies, education and training initiatives
- recorded instructions – CD ROM and multimedia, technical procedures
- recorded announcements – public address systems, in-store announcements, telephone messaging, safety instructions, inflight or train announcements
- storytelling – books on tape, animation, computer games.

Working as a voice-over artist can be a full-time career in its own right. There are several books dedicated to this subject, and they are thorough in their observation and guidance of how to read copy. Here is a brief outline of what the job entails in the context of you, the TV presenter. (*See* also Chapter 4 for vocal exercises.)

ESSENTIAL SKILLS

Initially, the majority of a TV presenter's voice-over work will be incorporated into the programme they are presenting as voicing reports or narrating action. Whatever the task, the following basic abilities are required. You need:

- to be able to leave all your daily anxieties or euphoria outside the studio, and relax the moment you arrive and pick up the script
- to be a great sight-reader and have the ability to maintain rapid communication between eye (the script and pictures), thought (the intention) and mouth (the speech)
- to have a resonant, clear voice with excellent diction
- to know *what* you sound like, not what you *think* you sound like – the two aren't always the same. Get used to hearing your voice and be objective about it
- to stop listening to yourself and get on with reading the script. If you are distracted by hearing yourself, try working with the cans only covering half of each ear
- to read the script in a conversational, natural manner
- to be able to hear in your head what the client or producer wants and vocally reproduce it
- to sound genuinely interested in 'Frasier's Better Bathrooms' and remain so during the 18th take
- to be able to deal with obscure direction such as, 'A little bit cosier with a brittle edge. You know, like the voice in that tyre advert!'
- to be able to fit a 40-second script into 30 seconds without cutting the script or sounding as if you're rushing through it
- to possess great timing and own an internal clock which can differentiate between 4 seconds and 4.5 seconds.

Technical know-how

Using a microphone
Try not to touch the microphone. Certainly, don't blow into it or tap it: whilst it won't do it any harm, it will really annoy the engineer and that's not someone you want to upset. Whether you are sitting or standing, make yourself physically comfortable. Most mics are positioned just a little to the side of the speaker's mouth or at forehead height, and allow for about a hand-span's distance between the mouth and the microphone. Always let the engineer adjust the mic and don't

re-adjust it once they've gone. You should be able to read your script easily without dropping or turning your head. Studio microphones are very sensitive and can register a difference in sound as you move.

You will always be asked for 'level'. Read a passage of the script at the same volume as you intend to read it for the recording. You may then be asked to back off the mic a fraction or come in a little closer. You don't have to stay locked into that position but remember where it was so that you can return to it when you start to record. All this is done for your benefit so that you are given every assistance to sound your best.

Many microphones have a 'pop stopper' or pop shield fixed to them to reduce the amount of air blasts. It happens most often with Ps and Bs and sometimes with Ts and 'who' (*see* also p.43).

Play to the mic. Even though you are not looking at it, relate to it as you would to a camera. Talk to your friend, one to one. Decide who it is you are talking to – it will help you to remain intimate and natural.

Headphones (cans)
Put them on as soon as you can. They put you in communication with the control room and allow you to hear yourself clearly. The volume of sound can be adjusted from the control box in the recording booth or from the main mixing desk by the sound engineer.

Cue lights
As mentioned above, you must be able to see the cue light clearly. It will flash on when you are required to speak – red or green are the usual colours. It is vital that you are prepared to react immediately: if you hesitate, the whole sequence may be out of synch. We are talking about fractions of seconds, and you must be able to come in on 'cue'. Anticipate the cue so that as the light comes on, you speak. Some producers will give you a verbal cue as well as a light. Agree with them, before you start, what their cue will be – 'Cue', 'Go', 'Read'.

Script
Don't lift the script up between you and the mic, and don't be a 'script rustler'. Put it safely on the desk or the script stand. Unclip any fastened pages so that page-turning can be done as noiselessly as possible. Have the pages separate; turning up the bottom right-hand corner can help. Turn the page only when you've finished speaking so that any paper rustle can be edited out later and won't interfere with your vocal recording.

Most voice-overs make notes on the pages to help their delivery. Take care not to over-mark your script so that you either can't see the original words or lose spontaneity and a natural flow as you read. The following are just some of the notations I use or have seen on other voice-overs' scripts.

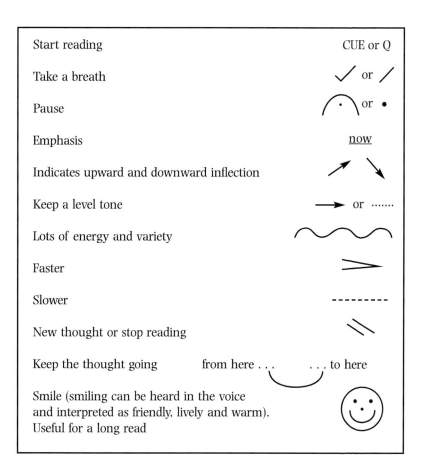

Start reading	CUE or Q
Take a breath	✓ or /
Pause	⌢• or •
Emphasis	<u>now</u>
Indicates upward and downward inflection	↗ ↘
Keep a level tone	→ or ·······
Lots of energy and variety	∼∼∼
Faster	⟩
Slower	- - - - - - - -
New thought or stop reading	⟍
Keep the thought going from here . . . . . . to here ⌣	
Smile (smiling can be heard in the voice and interpreted as friendly, lively and warm). Useful for a long read	☺

WORDS AND PICTURES

Very often the video which you are voicing will be shown on a monitor in a recording booth. From the visuals you can sense very quickly the style and feel of the read. The danger is to let the pictures do the talking and not engage yourself in the story. It's not simply a matter of speaking the text, but of fitting the words – and in some cases the emotional response

– to the pictures. Putting the right name to the right face and the correct description with the appropriate action requires good timing. And in order to ensure that your timing is accurate, you will need to anticipate cues. As well as a light cue or verbal cue from the producer you'll see a time code at the bottom of the screen. It registers hours, minutes, seconds and frames (24 frames in a second): e.g. 02:45:30:00. On an agreed cue you should speak immediately. Communication between eye, thought and mouth must be instantaneous.

A PRACTICAL CHECK-LIST

- Be vocally warmed up.
- Be prepared for work with everything you need close at hand.
- Keep some still water near by.
- Make yourself comfortable and relaxed.
- Be certain that the microphone is at the correct height for you, cue lights are in clear vision and that you are happy with all sound levels.
- Mark your script to assist your performance and delivery.
- Turn off mobile phones.

VOCAL INTERPRETATION

Whatever you are given to voice, it's your task to make the words come alive. Anyone can read words on a page, but the voice-over makes the words sound natural, as though talking to someone close by. Some voice-overs describe this as 'connecting'. Be friendly and talk to, not at, the listener. Your task is not to read but to communicate, making the words your own and totally believing, for that moment, in what you are saying. It's almost as if you have to pretend that the script isn't there.

DEMO TAPE OR SHOWREEL

Your demonstration tape is your introduction to agents, radio stations, advertising agencies and voice-over producers. This may be your only chance to get in through the door, so – as with your presenter's showreel (*see* also pp.162-6) – it's worth spending time and money on its presentation and content. It's surprising how many people just edit a few pieces together without too much thought. This is a great shame, since it's a perfect opportunity to make an impression. The following are suggestions to help improve your chances.

- Keep it short – a maximum of 3 minutes in total. Producers don't have time to listen to longer demos.
- Each extract should be short and sweet, some as short as 5 seconds. Cross-mix, fade in and out, edit clips together. Use pieces you've already done if you have them, or re-record them. Alternatively, write your own.
- Begin with your strongest, most marketable voice. You'll find this is the easiest one to do, since 99% of the time it will be your natural voice. Most producers only listen to the first 15–30 seconds unless they are really hooked by what you do.
- Stick to a realistic voice without fancy reverb and effects, certainly for the first two or three extracts. It's your *voice* they want to hear, not the amazing studio production.
- Don't use styles you'll never be cast for. For instance, if you have a gentle, soft and smoky sound, reading the hard-sell advert 'All carpets must go!' won't work.
- If you can afford it, use professional recording equipment or hire a studio. Print your showreel on to a CD rather than a cassette tape. A quality CD will attract quality work. Design a personalised presentation cover, and make it look professional. Present yourself as a professional. Don't sell yourself cheap.

EXERCISES

(1) Find a holiday brochure. Read aloud an advert or promotion. Record yourself.
Take a look at the advert again. Imagine the sounds behind the picture. Close your eyes and put yourself in the picture. Now read and record the advert again.
Do the same with a car magazine, gardening magazine or a food magazine.

(2) Read an extract from a holiday article, or current affairs or technical guide, as if narrating to pictures. Visualise clearly.

WHAT THEY SAY

'A voice-over needs to be able to respond to direction. And timing is crucial, fitting the words in and making sense of them in the time available. I look for a voice that stands out through accent or individual personality.'
Kevin Wooldridge (SKY TV)

'Using presenters for voicing commercials can be quite difficult. You'd think that they'd be used to reading text, but they leave words off the end of sentences, even if they're written in the script. The relaxed approach works in conversation but in voice-over every word has to count. It has to be accurate.'
David Lucas (Thames FM commercial producer)

'It's vital that when you first look at a copy, you familiarise yourself with it, read it several times and understand the main points so that you will be able to read it with conviction and comprehension. Ask yourself, "What is the point of this paragraph? What are the key words?" You have to make an emotional connection between yourself and what you are saying. You have to believe it. Good voices have good imaginations.'
Peter Dickson (voice-over artist)

'You can earn good money as a voice-over, but like all jobs, the clients and agents want someone nice to work with. It requires a great deal of concentration and you must listen carefully to all directions and comments over the talkback. Some of them may be derogatory – especially from clients who don't understand that you can hear their every word if the talkback is open. Don't worry about it – just pick up on what they're trying to achieve.

When it comes down to it, this profession is 50% having a great voice and using it correctly and 50% being wonderful to work with. If you remember this salient fact you won't go far wrong.'
The Excellent Voice Company

19

The Game-Show Host

It's party-time! Fun! Jokey! Relaxed! Informal! Witty repartee! Innuendo! Chaos! A game show can decline as quickly as that unless the host remains disciplined and in control. The majority of programmes are recorded live, in front of a studio audience, giving a sense of immediacy and excitement to the show. They will only be stopped if something goes drastically wrong – either technically, as in the Wheel of Fortune getting stuck, or verbally, as in a presenter giving away the answer or swearing. Crazy, madcap game shows only work because they are well rehearsed, technically co-ordinated, and in the hands of a group of people expert at keeping control. If they were as chaotic and seemingly ad hoc as they appear on the screen, then chances are that it might all go horribly wrong. When TV stations or programme producers are spending money, nothing is left to mere chance; it's a risk they will not take. But when the cameras roll, it's your responsibility to keep the show moving and not be distracted by the crew, guests or remarks from the gallery. Of course, you should have fun and enjoy yourself, but keep that inner energy and drive focused.

Game shows have been described as 'utterly compelling' and 'fascinating human drama'. They are about people, and the best presenters seem to have a genuine rapport with the contestants. A lot of game shows are hosted by stand-up comics, and certainly many hosts have some sort of comedy background. That's not only because they are commercially good value, bringing their own audience with them, but also because they are used to the unexpected. They are able to keep going through all kinds of rough waters whilst remaining entertaining and in control. Some gentler panel games are hosted by ex-newsreaders or former radio presenters – people who are skilled at asking questions, listening to panellists, listening to talkback and chatting to the viewer at the same time. What all these presenters share, as TV presenter and game-show host Cheryl Baker says, is 'honesty, professionalism, genuine interest and a good sense of humour'.

TV presenter Philip Schofield claims that the secret of hosting game shows is knowing every conceivable way that the game can play out. In other words, being totally prepared for anything. The essential ingredient that will always take you by surprise, and will always be unpredictable, is the contestant. There is no way that you can predict what they will do or say when the show starts. They have been interviewed, auditioned and selected for the show for their personality and potential entertainment value. In many cases they are chosen to compliment the style of the presenter for the best possible interaction. Ultimately, the contestants are in your care, in your environment. You are the host of a great party, and how you exploit a situation in which a contestant either clams up with nerves or gets hysterical as the game progresses will make or break your show. Be ready for unguarded remarks which can feed a clever one-line retort or facial reaction. There are game shows which incorporate celebrity guests, allowing them to bring their own brand of humour and entertainment to the show. Give them space to do just that. Sections of script may be written for them: be prepared to accommodate them.

Enjoyment is a key ingredient of the game show, but there has to be a winner and a loser. The joy of winning is infectious but no one likes to lose. Try to remember the importance of this day for the contestants, who have been dreaming about it for weeks. Their hopes are high, and when they walk away empty-handed – their pride hurt in front of thousands of people, many of whom are colleagues and friends – they will need your diplomatic and sympathetic support so that they can leave with good grace. Practically, time is limited and you will have to get them off the set and move on with the game as quickly as you can. But try to soften the blow with a consolation prize and the tried and tested lines, 'You've been great contestants and we're really pleased you came. Have you enjoyed your day here on *Cross Your Fingers?*' Close the show with an upbeat feel, thanking one and all.

SOME HELPFUL HINTS

- Concentrate on the programme; take control and remain in control.
- Sign clearly who you are talking to. Make sure that you know each contestant's name.
- Be actively involved in directing the audience's attention and helping the director mix shots, by smooth indication rather than jumping from guest to guest.
- Talk to the contestants and the studio audience as well as to the camera.
- Include the audience at home. Involve everyone in the game.
- Have fun!

20

The TV Commentator

The popular perception of the TV commentator is one of a reporter in a sheepskin coat, headphones firmly locked in place over their ears and leaning so close to a microphone that it's nearly wedged between their front teeth. However, it is a skilled job, and one that is almost always given to someone with a specialist knowledge of the event being covered. That might be anything from a sporting gala to a fashion show, aerial display, royal pageant or political event. In short, the commentator will be present wherever an activity is being broadcast.

The commentator will usually cover a live event, sometimes providing a voice-over which is added to the film at a later date. As SKY sports presenter Suzi Perry says, 'It's completely different from TV presenting. You are commentating on what you are *seeing*.' In a live situation the TV commentator has to think on their feet and report the action as it happens, interpret the action and identify the people and players. You are the senses of the viewer and, with little or no script at all, it is your task to verbally recreate the atmosphere.

Since you are involved in the action, and in an ideal situation to recount the whole experience, it's important that your knowledge of the event is excellent – and that no matter what your own preferences, you remain impartial. For fast-moving sporting action, sentences should be short and language simple yet appropriate to the event. Of course, there may be times in the excitement of the moment when you will need to rein in your natural enthusiasm and find a level where you can still be vocally understood, but it's vital that all times you keep up with the pace of the action. When a more measured pace is required your language can become more expressive and you can use any visual references as an opportunity to further colour your commentary. The trick is to know when to keep silent and let the action speak for itself. This is probably the key point of good commentating. It can happen that there is a lull in the proceedings, in which case you can access your library of interesting facts and anecdotes.

21

The Weather Reporter

To be a weather reporter, it is not essential to have an expansive meteo-rological knowledge – but you will need to have a basic understanding of weather patterns in order to explain their effect convincingly. The viewer will expect you to know what you are talking about. Information can be found on the news information services (known as the wires). Time is short for these reports, generally between 30 seconds and a maximum of 3 minutes. This is because there is enormous pressure on the whole news section to finish on time, and weather is either used as a slot to absorb extra time or trimmed to fit the schedule. Since the length of your report can change within seconds of going on air, you will need to have plenty of extra information and be able to ad lib as necessary, as well as an ability to cut short your report at a moment's notice. Because of this it's less common to use an autocue; some presenters stick a cue sheet close up against the camera.

Each station has its own style of weather reporting, but essentially the viewer will just want the facts – whether it is going to rain or not, or what the temperature is likely to be. As you create your report it will be useful to have a clear understanding of the geography of the weather map and the current pattern of the weather. Begin with a general view of the weather as it is, noting any areas of major change. Follow the movement of the weather pattern as it affects the area you are concerned with. Try not to jump from area to area – if the change is coming from the west, start in the west. Take the viewer on a journey of the weather, tracking the projected weather change and its effects. If you have time at the end, give a brief summary. Add in a 3-day forecast if you have it, but be wary of using absolutes – weather patterns can change. Temperatures are given in Celsius but it's entirely up to you how you refer to them: for instance, 22; 22 degrees; 22 degrees Celsius. You may also wish to include the equivalent in Fahrenheit.

More often than not you will be using a chroma key (*see* also Chapter 16, pp. 117-22). You will be in control of switching weather maps by using a button hand switch. Anticipate the changes so that there is no break in your delivery. Using chroma key, or a drop in graphic (as used in Channel 5 TV weather reports), you will only be able to see the maps on the output monitor. Make sure that the monitor is in your peripheral vision so that you are not tempted to look directly at it. Although it's easier to face the chroma-key screen as you talk, try to turn to it only as you indicate a particular area (but make sure that you always turn back to the viewer).

- *Physically* – connect with the viewer using open body language. Keep fairly still. The shot is likely to be static and tight. At the same time, try to achieve a relaxed, fluid movement as you turn to and from the camera. Stand up straight and indicate clearly. Look after your hands and nails. Maintain an energy in your fingers – do not allow them to curl, or your wrists to flop limply.
- *Vocally* – keep your voice alert and full of energy. Colour each phrase. Bring a fresh energy to each new piece of information. There's no need to be too serious, these are facts which you can have an opinion about. Finish with a smile, facing the camera.

EXERCISE
Look at the sample weather report below, then create your own 40-second weather bulletin using the following information.

Today – partly cloudy. Wind from north-west bringing more cloud and rain. Becoming windy, especially across more hilly areas. Southern areas fairly dry at the start. Showers expected later. Temperatures 10–15 degrees.

Overnight – wind gathering speed. Possible gales in south-east and heavy rain or blustery showers. Temperatures near normal for the time of year at 8–9 degrees.

Tomorrow – clearing from west. Plenty of sunshine, fairly windy. Followed by more rain. Temperatures unexpectedly warm at 15–16 degrees.

SAMPLE WEATHER REPORT

SCRIPT 1
SHOT 1. CAM 1. MLS PRES. WEATHER AREA. CK CAM
OVER MAP   / SOUND

| ITEM 8 WEATHER | | |
| PRESENTER | It's a grey and misty start to the day, but that will give way to sunny | STUDIO |

SUPER
PAMELA
spells and warmer weather throughout the whole of the British Isles –
although in Northern Ireland and
Northern Scotland the early fog will
take longer to clear. Maximum
temperatures 13–16 degrees lowering
to 7 degrees overnight. The outlook is
increasingly good with more
sunshine and warmer temperatures.
That's all from me until 12 noon.
Have a good morning.

WHAT THEY SAY

'Always tell the story, that's what the best presenters do. Chat to the viewer. The weather can change very quickly and we don't always get it right. I like to refer to it if it was completely wrong; it shows that we're human. The hardest part is talking to time.

There is no visual aid other than the monitor to show you what you are talking about, so if it goes wrong, everything is crazy. That's where your training comes in: that's what you are paid for.'
Siân Lloyd (ITN Weather)

'At very short notice I was screen-tested to cover for the regular weather guy. I knew nothing about the weather, though I'd spent so much time watching others I'd kind of picked it up. I've since become really interested in it. You learn very quickly what people need to know and what they don't.

It's beautiful presenting on the roof of the building: you feel that you are actually engaging, connecting with what you are talking about. Doing the weather report is like a relay race. It's as though I've been handed a blazing torch or a baton – I have a few moments with it, on air, and then I pass it on to someone else.'
Jeff Moody (Channel 5 Weather)

22

The Travel Reporter

Traffic information comes from the police, motoring associations and the public. Any information given by the public should be verified; alternatively, acknowledge that it is only an eyewitness account and not official data. Reports may well include public transport information and any airline news.

Very little time is given for this slot so your report has to be as precise and concise as possible. Give just the facts. The viewer wants to know *where* there is a problem, *why* there is a delay and *how long* it is likely to last. They are looking out for news of their particular route and any problems that will affect them. Therefore, it's important that you identify the troubled area first and then stress road names, junctions, approach roads and affected directions such as clockwise, anti-clockwise, northbound, southbound and so on. If there's a ring road, give information in a clockwise direction. Create a natural route map for your report, rather than randomly hopping from one trouble spot to another. Depending on the flow of traffic and time of day – for instance, the rush hour – you can start from within the city centre or the approach roads. However, you should mention any serious travel problem first.

The viewer will also want to know if the congestion you mentioned earlier has cleared up. If you have enough transmission time then include it, but you'll have to use your discretion on this one. If there are no major traffic problems, give a general overview and then start on specifics such as roadworks.

- *Physically* – keep your body fairly still. It's pure facts that are required from you and not distracting body language. If you are using maps or local traffic cameras, refer to them with open gestures.
- *Vocally* – keep your voice bright and energised. Be interested in what you are saying and concerned, suggesting an understanding of how frustrating this must be or sharing the general relief that all roads are clear.

EXERCISES

(1) Read and present the following script.

SHOT 1 CAM 1 MCU PRES. STUDIO   /

ITEM 1   No major problems to report so far this
                  afternoon, but on the M63 exit for Sale,
                  Junction 7, watch out for a traffic build-up as
                  there are major roadworks on the Chester
                  Road.
                  – The M62 at Prestwich is now all clear after
                  an earlier accident.
                  – And local diversions have now been lifted
                  around Belle Vue Street in West Gorton
                  following emergency repairs to a burst water
                  main, although traffic is down to one lane.
                  – An early reminder that this weekend it's
                  carnival time, so the city centre will be very
                  busy, especially around Whitworth Street,
                  Sackville Street and Princess Street.
                  My name is .... and
                  I'll be bringing you a travel update on the
                  hour, every hour from *Traffic Watch*.

(2) Choose a local event and imagine the travel implications.
       Are there any transport alternatives such as buses, park-
       and-ride facilities? If there was a jack-knifed lorry
       obstructing a main access road, how would that affect
       traffic? Write and present your report (duration 30 seconds,
       45 seconds or 1 minute).

Part Four

CORPORATE PRESENTING

23

The Corporate World
on Camera

Efficiency in business relies on clear and fast communication. At one time the corporate world on camera was restricted to an occasional video presentation or rare appearance of a company spokesman on TV, usually caught in the headlamps of some crisis. However, technology is evolving so quickly that more advanced and effective systems are constantly becoming available. Communications media vary greatly, as do environments for presentation: corporate training on video, satellite link-up to conference venues and live presentations transmitted to large presentation screens; video telephony and video conferencing; network and cable broadcasts; Internet and Intranet. Never before has the business world been so exposed or so accountable, with individual executives and their companies now being judged on how well they present themselves.

It's clear that business etiquette and presentation play a vital role in day-to-day management, and these elements should not be ignored as the user becomes more at ease with the technology. The good news is that the corporate presenter doesn't need to know all the technical aspects of the system being used, just how to get the best out of it and how to develop their abilities as a communicator across all media. It is easy to be distracted by all the gadgetry and sideline the most important and effective communication tool – *you*. This is the time to put yourself in focus. Many of the basic principles of TV presentation apply to the corporate world, but it's worthwhile taking time in this chapter to recap on areas that are particularly relevant, as well as address some of the various technologies currently in use.

THE PRESENTERS

Although sharing many of the same skills and techniques, TV presenters and corporate presenters have different aims. The corporate presenter's very clear objective is to reflect company business, regardless of whether they are a professional presenter working predominantly in business conferencing – adopting the mantle of a corporate figure without being an employee of that company – or the business executive who uses screen communication and is actually part of the company. Whilst TV presenting skills apply to both, there is a slight difference in preparation, see the 'W' checklist, p.149

The professional presenter

A celebrity TV presenter is sometimes asked to host a live conference or a promotional or training video. In such a situation there is no point in pretending to be a company employee: you have been employed for your TV personality and everyone knows it. However, you do have a responsibility to make your presentation as relevant to your audience as you can. Incorporate any information and anecdotes you are given about the company and the personnel. Occasionally the script will be written for you, but you will still need to infuse it with your own style and humour.

Some companies like the idea of using an anonymous figure to host or present their conferences. They have no hidden agenda; they can add a touch of class; and they take the pressure off the main speakers by making smooth introductions and chairing the event.

There are professional presenters who make a good living out of just presenting corporate events and videos. It's their responsibility to understand the thought-processes and image of the corporate world so that they are seen as a credible presenter. As with the celebrity, it's unwise to pretend that you are a company employee, but having as much information as possible suggests that you are representing the organisation both knowledgeably and sympathetically. To maintain credibility, I recommend fully researching the assigned company and the subject matter.

The professional presenter will frequently be asked for input, and perhaps to write their own introductions and closing lines. Actors are also used in promotional and training videos, and it can save time and money to use those professional presenters and actors who are able to learn scripts and make sense of the most complicated procedures and methodology. There is one skill which I have only seen professional presenters use, and for it to be effective it requires hours of practice and a great deal of expertise. Faced with a long, complicated script which needs to be filmed in one sequence – usually on location – the presenter will pre-record the script using a mini-recorder. With the aid of an earpiece they will use the tape as an aide memoire, speaking one word behind the audio reply. Performed with sufficient skill to appear totally natural, this can be a very useful ability.

The business executive as presenter

This presenter usually has a strong message to communicate, whether that is to sell something, to inform, to educate or motivate. Before dealing with the different media that the corporate presenter is likely to encounter, it's worthwhile covering the basic principles of corporate presentation and defining 'you, the presenter' in terms of your message and your company. Your key aims are to:

- communicate
- deliver a clear message
- present yourself, the company and the product in the best possible light.

First, let's take a look at 'you, the corporate presenter'. Any acting or showmanship will be seen as phoney and your business will appear untrustworthy. Be sincere, natural, candid, genuine and straightforward – these are the qualities that a corporate viewer positively responds to. Be honest with yourself. To identify yourself, try the exercises in Chapter 2, pp. 5-10. Answer the questions with you and your business in mind. Do you know your personal business attributes and those of your company?

EXERCISES

(1)   Write down a list of events that you have presented or spoken at in the last two or three years. They may be professional or social – family events, neighbourhood committees or prize givings. Circle those presentations where you felt most comfortable, and ask yourself why you think that was.

Is there anything you can take from the most comfortable

situation and use in the less comfortable situation?
It may be that you were amongst friends or that you knew
what you were talking about. Refer to Chapter 5 on Fighting
Fears, and use any of the exercises to strengthen your
confidence.

(2) Write down your job description.

_____

_____

Then write down 4 or 5 valuable qualities which you possess
and make you good at your job. I am:

(a) _____

(b) _____

(c) _____

(d) _____

(e) _____

Face a blank wall and read them out loud.
Do it again and say it louder, this time with pride.

(3) Face a blank wall. You may sit or stand. Focus on a spot at
eye-level where you can envisage a camera lens. Imagine a
supportive colleague or someone for whom you have mutual
respect, and place their image in the lens. Tell them the
following:
Say your name. State your role in the company and spend
about a minute on your favourite pastime. Explain why you
enjoy it.
Now, using a video camera, repeat the exercise. As you
review it take into account all the information you have
already read in this book regarding posture, body language,
energy and commitment. Note how in the section on your
pastime you relax and are more conversational. Try to find a
balance between your professional stance and the more
relaxed approach for your next presentation.
At times you may want to be more assured in your delivery
to camera. Try the exercise again, this time with a more
assertive attitude. Record and review. How do you react as a
viewer? Try to be objective!

THE PRESENTATION

Every presenter and every presentation will be different. The following questions are extremely useful as a check-list for every presentation, no matter what medium you are using.

The 'W' checklist

- *What* is the purpose of this presentation? This is probably the most important of all the questions. It underpins every aspect of your delivery. If you know what the core message is then you can shape your presentation accordingly.
- *What* key points do you want them to know?
- *Who* are you talking to? Do they have any preconceived ideas about your work or about you? What do they know? It's important to pitch your presentation at the appropriate level. Too much jargon or over-simplification will alienate your viewer.
- *What* do they want to know? Are there any main issues that should be addressed? Will they be interested in every detail or do you need to review your text?
- *What* do you *not* want to tell them? You can be sure that if you don't identify these points, somehow they will slip out. Mark them clearly in your mind.
- *Why* are you making this speech? Why you and not someone else? Is it because of your status, your expertise, your specialised knowledge? You've worked hard and earned the right to speak up, now be proud of it.
- *Where* are you making the presentation? Is it on familiar territory? If not, find ways to make yourself at ease. Try out the chair and walk around in the space you will be working in.
- *What* is the expected duration of the communication? Don't waste time. Make sure that you have clear objectives.
- *What* form of communication are you using? Choose ones that enhance and don't hinder your presentation. Choose media that complement your presentation.

Follow the 'W' check-list with the four Rs:
- *Recognise* – the objectives for making this communication, personal and business; the speaker support requirements, technical and environmental.
- *Rehearse* – read through your notes and speak them aloud; practise names and phrases that are difficult to pronounce.
- *Record.*
- *Review.*

Giving the right impression

Image

Remember the importance of initial contact. The image we see on screen has an immediate effect on how we go on to interpret verbal information – and the first visual impression is lasting. If you haven't already done so, try re-reading Chapter 3 with your business image in mind, and applying some of the practical tips to your corporate presentation.

In assessing your image you don't have to reinvent yourself: you only need to judge how best to reveal the strongest qualities that you already possess. It's a balance of being at ease and promoting a personal image that is compatible with your company image or presentation. Perhaps you are used to slouching or fiddling with your pen, but now want to give the impression of positively engaging in the task at hand. It may take time to make the changes, and they may feel uncomfortable at first – but small adjustments will soon become natural behaviour. A simple haircut may not feel so different to you but may make a world of difference to your colleagues. They'll say, 'It's a new you.' And that's what it should be – a new you, not a different one. As you match your outward appearance with your personal ambitions and drive, you will feel more confident and your presentation and message will be far more convincing.

EXERCISES

(1) Stand in front of a full-length mirror. Take a look at yourself, observing your height, weight and colouring.
Now take a more detailed look. Observe your hair, make-up, jewellery and watch, style of clothing and shoes. Is there any part of your look that you don't feel comfortable with or that doesn't promote the desired image? Could you change that aspect with a bit of effort?

(2) Observe your posture. In front of a long mirror, pull up a chair and observe how you sit.
Try sitting with different postures and judge for yourself what attitude you are conveying.
- Sit upright, bottom tucked into the back to the chair.
- Sit upright, bottom tucked into the back to the chair, and lean forwards.
- Sit on the edge of the chair and lean forwards.
- Sit on the edge of the chair and lean back in a relaxed manner.
- Sit in the position you feel most comfortable in.

The start and finish

The start and finish of any presentation have a considerable effect on how you are perceived and what is remembered afterwards. Each encounter will necessitate a different approach, but it is valuable to remember a few general points.

- Introduce yourself clearly and positively. Let your name mean something. Start the meeting with an open posture and relaxed demeanour. Exude confidence.
- Finish on a positive note. No matter what the content of your presentation or conversation, gather your thoughts together, summarise if possible and confidently allude to further research, the next meeting, or future developments. Don't let your voice trail away. Say goodbye, be polite and make it clear that the meeting is finished.

Vocal impact

As you have no control over the sound system through which your voice will be heard, clarity of tone and diction are all-important. The pace of your delivery needs to be monitored: too fast, and you won't be understood; too slow and you'll be boring. Listen to yourself on the system you will be using or on a similar one. Record your speech if you can, and play it back. Note your energy level. By simply committing yourself to what you are saying you will stop mumbling and repeating downward inflections. Be direct and use motivational language, making the most of descriptive words and imagery. Refer to the exercises in Chapter 4, or get expert advice from a voice coach. Here's a useful check-list:

- Warm up your voice before you begin. Practise articulation exercises.
- Do some simple physical stretches.
- Give energy to the first word.
- Use vocal variety and a range of notes.
- Use visual imagery and enjoy adjectives.
- Don't speak too fast or too slow.
- Maintain your energy throughout the communication.

APPEARING IN A CORPORATE VIDEO

Conducting a presentation on video gives you the luxury of delivering a carefully considered message. With thorough preparation it can be honed to a high standard, covering all the integral points. Remind yourself of the 'W' checklist (*see* p. 149).

Facing a camera for the first time can be quite daunting. Try to relax and remember that the film crew are there to help you look and sound good – they are not sitting in judgement of you. Just forget about them and trust the director, who can often see what works and what doesn't. If you are courageous enough to accept their advice and constructive criticism you can benefit from the experience.

Use your time effectively

The corporate video can be filmed almost anywhere the client chooses, and very often a presenter will choose to use their own office. Wherever you are, concentrate on the one task of filming – any other business concerns can wait. Distractions diffuse your energy and add to nervous tension. As far as the viewer is concerned you are talking to them one-on-one, so give them 100% of your attention. Turn your phone off as soon as you begin rehearsals.

Prepare to present

Talk *to* the camera, not *at* it. Put the image of a supportive colleague or friend in the camera lens and talk to them, personally. Even if your video presentation is to be shown to several hundred delegates at a conference, they are still individuals and need to be addressed as such. Tell them the story, talk naturally, inspire and enthuse. If you trip up over a few words, keep going. To the viewer it can appear very natural but, if a fluff really worries you, remember that you can re-record that section later. If you keep stopping and starting, correcting and re-correcting yourself you will lose the momentum and flow.

Rehearsing at home is always advisable. It helps you to relax and achieve a comfortable rhythm. But be aware of over-rehearsing to the point where you can lose touch with the subject matter. Rehearsing in the studio or on set is just as important: becoming familiar with this unnatural environment will help you feel more at ease. Occasionally a presenter will say, 'Let's just do it in one,' but in my experience this can leave everyone feeling rather short-changed. It's a rare presentation that could not have been improved with a second or third take. Also, if you believe in your message you will want to commit time to it. Remember that the camera can read your real intentions and a throw-away speech or authoritarian manner speaks volumes.

Try to have the camera at head-height so that you are at eye-level with your viewer and not imperiously looking down on them or subserviently looking upwards. (The exception to this is when you are filming on location, and you are presenting from up on a gantry or down a well, for example. The aim of such a shot would be to capture the environment and not to comment on your status.) A presentation delivered straight to camera and filmed in a static office location may be valuable when making a vital and serious point, but it will not hold the attention of your audience for very long. If you are totally comfortable with your presentation and with your message, you and the director can be more creative in making the video more interesting to watch. This shouldn't involve gimmicky camera shots which distract from your message, but slight changes in framing and different camera techniques such as hand-held filming or tracking shots. These can have a strong visual impact if you are confident with your presentation.

CONFERENCE AND SATELLITE LINK-UP

For any conference meeting, the accomplished presenter should have public-speaking skills and arrive at the venue personally prepared and professionally rehearsed. At large events using video screens and satellite link-up, the presenter should concentrate solely on their presentation and not be overly concerned with the technology. Many presenters believe that because they have powerful microphones, and because the presentation is being transmitted to video screens, they need only give an intimate TV performance. In fact, where you have a live audience and simultaneous transmission to a large screen, the presentation has to be 'larger' than might feel natural. Movement and gestures should be clear and defined; strong, not mean and small. The voice needs projection and articulation. Speak clearly but you don't need to shout.

When using a satellite link-up, be aware that there may be a slight delay in transmission. Have the confidence to wait, and be advised by the technical crew. Always talk to the image of the person you are connecting with, even though they may not have an image of you and the conference.

VIDEO CONFERENCING

This is an increasingly popular mode of business communication with a wide scope. Video conferencing enables people to hold prepared or spontaneous meetings, sharing information and establishing visual contact without being in the same room, building or even country. Furthermore, using streaming capabilities the entire meeting or presentation can be watched in real time or stored and viewed later by authorised personnel equipped with a web browser.

Video conferencing (courtesy of AuDeo Systems Ltd)

The current scope of video conferencing ranges from individual, face-to-face video desk phones to PC- or appliance-based systems with connecting microphone and camera, to much bigger, stand-alone systems linking one or more stations to a large conference meeting hall. Huge events with video satellite link-ups mean that a conference can take place simultaneously across the world with active participation by delegates at various sites. Larger equipment has high-resolution cameras with zoom and panning facilities, and multi-directional microphones – some with extensions to allow participants to move freely about the conference space.

CAUGHT ON CAMERA

Nothing will replace human contact and the close-proximity readings of body language and physical chemistry, which is why many people find video conferencing impersonal and distant. The videophone usually frames only a mid-shot (waist up), a medium close-up (head and shoulders) or a close-up (head and neck). Try to keep your head relatively still or it will fall out of shot. On most office systems the camera is situated above the screen. The effect of this is that if you look at the person you are talking to, your eyeline will also be directed downwards. You can remedy this by looking at the camera lens when you are listening to the caller, for as much of the time as you can. Of course, you will want to look at the caller for reaction and reassurance, so practise slowly lowering your eyes as if in thought.

You usually have the option to see an image of yourself in the corner. Try not to watch yourself or be distracted by your own picture; use it purely for reference. It's useful to see what the caller is seeing, and to make sure that you are in the camera frame.

The remote control capability of many conferencing stations means that it's possible both to capture the whole group and to focus on individuals. So, a participant in one location can focus on another in a separate location, whether they are talking or not. Gone are the days when you could sit in a meeting without saying a word and hope you wouldn't be noticed. As with the videophone, your relationship with all participants should be direct and focused. It's interesting to note that whilst the camera doesn't pick up all the subliminal signs that we acknowledge in personal contact, it does magnify many other reactions, responses and attitudes. Refer back to the 'W' checklist and check your role and purpose for being at this video conference.

IMAGE AND ENVIRONMENT

What are you wearing? Is it an image you feel comfortable with and want to be 'caught on camera' in? Remember to avoid checks and striped patterns.

Choose your location well. Your surroundings will say more about you than perhaps you want to disclose. How distracting is the wallpaper? Are you in an open office? Be conscious of any action behind you and re-position your system accordingly. Are there any books, papers or graphics that you wouldn't want a caller to see?

Plain white walls can make you look very pale, and a change in lighting can reduce that effect. Do, however, make sure that you are well lit. If there is too much light from the windows, close the blinds or change your position. A background of solid colour is preferable.

BANDWIDTH

How your image is received is dependent on transmission and receiving capabilities. The connection between PCs is mainly via LAN (Local Area Network), ISDN (Integrated Services Digital Network), ADSL (Asyncronis Digital Signal Link) or cable. These are communication channels, and they need to have a big enough *bandwidth* to be able to carry pictures and video. The bandwidth refers to the amount of data that can be moved down a telephone line or other network. It's extremely common to see fragmented pictures and jerky movement: this is caused by insufficient bandwidth.

The bigger the bandwidth, the more information can be sent and the better the quality of sound and picture. Pictures are translated into tiny dots (pixels) which re-configure at their destination. Travelling at lower than 30 frames per second the picture begins to break up, so that any movement appears to be jerky. Such degradation of sound and motion applies on the Internet, too, especially during busy times and when the server is heavily loaded. As you cannot guarantee that the recipient of your call or transmission will have high-standard equipment, keep all movements as smooth and gentle – but also as natural – as possible.

ETIQUETTE

On an ordinary phone you can dryly answer a number or curtly say 'Hello'. On the video phone you are immediately sending visual messages. Your initial contact makes a lasting impression and can set the tone for the entire meeting, so begin your dialogue on a positive and receptive note. When you receive the call, be welcoming. Refrain from reacting as though someone has irritatingly interrupted you. Be sure too that you monitor other calls coming in so that you are not disturbed unnecessarily.

SOME TIPS FOR PRESENTING (VIDEO PHONE AND VIDEO CONFERENCING)

- Prepare well in advance. Have all the necessary information to hand, and make notes of all the points you wish to cover.
- Practise with a home video.
- Ask your caller if they can hear and see you clearly. You can then modify movement and speech accordingly.
- Maintain direct and focused contact; eye contact is always important.
- Avoid closed gestures. Limit movement.
- If you are about to move out of the camera shot, tell your caller.
- Don't over-relax. This is still a business meeting.
- Don't talk over each other, especially in groups.
- Keep alert at all times, even if you're not speaking.
- Aim for vocal variety in pitch.
- Keep a brightness of sound in your voice. Speak clearly.
- Be aware of any tension showing in your face, and smile when you can.

INTERNET AND INTRANET

The Internet reaches a worldwide audience and is accessible to everyone, while Intranet is accessible within a company structure with a more specific agenda. Presentations and communications need to reflect these differences, in both style and content. As the computer monitor screen is small, and very often the filmed sequence will appear in the corner of that screen amongst text, the best shot will be a tightly trained close-up against a solid colour background. Most transmissions are pre-recorded or filmed as live, then stored and downloaded at the viewer's convenience. However, it is possible to view in real time: this is known as webcasting. Bloomberg LP broadcast simultaneously over the Internet and on cable TV. The quality of moving pictures on the Internet varies with the receiving capabilities of each system, and it's worth noting that the audio is often clearer than the picture. As the sender, though, there is little you can do to assist – vocally over-compensating can make you sound stern and emphatic. Stick with the fundamental rules of presenting to camera: maintain clear objectives, economical movement and a clear vocal delivery.

Websites

Clear images and clear messages are vital on a website. Choose three points you want to make and work on those. You need to use a marketing strategy, defining your purpose and recognising audience needs. Filmed sequences attract attention, but be sure they are easily accessible and if possible provide a facility to download the correct player. Select still images and suitable videos which reinforce your message. When filming a piece to camera that is specifically for a website, employ the same presentation techniques as you would when filming a corporate video.

TEXT AND GRAPHIC PRESENTATION

Just as script and props are vital for the TV presenter, so the corporate presenter needs to have excellent visual aids. Remember, however, that whilst impressive applications can transform proposals and presentations, too much technical wizardry can actually detract from the message.

Here are some basic guidelines for preparing any visual speaker support.

- KISS (Keep It Short and Simple). What is your main message?
- Use strong visual impact. Use simple images which directly relate to your presentation.

- Graphs and diagrams with boxes, triangles and arrows should be logical and drawn clearly.
- Choose colours carefully. It's sometimes difficult to differentiate from a distance. Too much colour coding can become confusing.

Text
- Use a maximum of 5 points only per side. There is no need to write up your whole speech.
- Use simple fonts, e.g. Helvetica or Arial.
- Avoid italics if you can.
- Use capitals and underlining sparingly; choose your main points.
- Size matters. Stand back from your monitor and judge for yourself how easy the text is to read. Use 18 or 24 pt for the main body of text, larger for any titles.

Attachments
Video clips and sound effects can sometimes be downloaded free from the Internet. There is plenty of software available to liven up your presentation, including cartoon figures, moving icons and 3D effects. Select wisely. Use something that enhances your presentation and your company but does not create a gimmicky advert.

WHAT THEY SAY

'For TV, the same rules of presentation apply – portray yourself. There is no difference between presenting to camera and presenting to a group of people. It might be a little unnerving to begin with, but whatever you say make it interesting and relevant to the audience. If there is slight delay with a satellite link-up, simply listen and wait for the response.'
Danny Coyle (The Imagination Group - Business TV)

'To maintain the attention of the viewer, it is very important that you have a high-powered message – but reciting company mantras and clichéd words is not acceptable. It's a conversation, and if you treat it like that you'll be fine.'
Paddy Hughes (Paddy Hughes Pictures)

'Internet capabilities are changing very quickly, offering companies untold opportunities. It's important that you use a good film company and pay attention to what you are saying in text, visual and audio.'
Anita Sharpe (CEO, Dash 30 and Pulitzer Prizewinner)

Part Five

GETTING THAT FIRST JOB

24

Getting Started

Theory is important but practice makes perfect. Unless you experiment, explore your own resources and actively perfect your craft, it really is just words. As you get to know your own voice, your own style and become familiar with presenting to a camera lens, you will feel more at ease when you attend a screen test or audition. Don't let your first appearance in a television studio be your last. So before you apply for any presenting job, rehearse and work on the exercises in this book. More than 10,000 hopeful presenters auditioned for BBC Talent[1] in 2000, and it was clear within 30 seconds who really wanted the job and who thought it might 'just be a fun thing to do'. If you don't take the vocation seriously you in turn will not be taken seriously. You have to show your enthusiasm and commitment to the job of being a TV presenter.

RESEARCH

In Chapter 2 we looked at the type of programmes you'd be most comfortable presenting. Start watching lots of similar programmes. Record

[1] A nationwide search for new talent in many areas of programme-making. Competition in all categories was fierce.

them on video so that you can see for yourself what works and what doesn't. What would you do or say in the same circumstances? Get yourself a note book and jot down useful phrases, introductions and out cues. You never know when they will come in handy.

Book yourself in as a member of the studio audience and watch a programme being filmed. It doesn't matter if it's a situation comedy, a quiz show or a chat show – any programme will do. Start familiarising yourself with the environment. Note all the technical goings on. Where's the floor manager? What hand signals do they give? How does the presenter prepare for the show? How do they maintain the momentum of the show and their own performance? Which camera is taking the shot? As well as the programme itself, there's plenty of action to watch. Clearly not all programmes have a studio audience, but you could write to the producer and try to persuade them to let you into the gallery. If you're already a journalist or a researcher you might find an appropriate article to write which necessitates watching a recording. Nothing ventured, nothing gained!

Keep an eye out for outside broadcasts. Look up sports events that are to be transmitted live, or TV road shows which are touring in your area. A word of warning, though: don't get into the camera shot and risk being a 'lurker'. In years to come, when you're a celebrity in your own right, you won't want that shot of you 'lurking' in the background or walking to and fro across camera coming back to haunt and embarrass you. Keep your distance!

COURSES

There are a number of relevant training courses advertised in trade magazines and broadsheets, ranging from intensive 3-day programmes to evening classes spread over a number of weeks. Most are quite expensive, so research and choose carefully. University media degrees offer a broad syllabus and a good foundation, but none can guarantee you a passport into the TV industry. (See pp. 168-9 for more information.)

GETTING STARTED

There are many ways to approach the world of TV presenting. Most often people come 'through the ranks' – in other words, they have worked as TV researchers, producers' assistants, runners, radio presenters and in other associated jobs. By taking on these varied career options, they not only gained insight and experience in the broadcasting world; they equipped themselves with valuable skills. The majority of news presenters are journalists: TV news programmes rarely employ people just to read the news. It may be in your interest to take a course in journalism or communication in the media. Without doubt, some journalistic experience is essential along with a clear understanding of current affairs. If your interest is more specific, for example: sport, business news, entertainment, health, then be an expert. Know your subject.

So where do you look to find the jobs? Well, you won't find them at the job centre! You may hear about an opening on the infamous 'grapevine' – simply put, by word of mouth. Or you may strike it lucky and land a job advertised in the local paper. Carol Vorderman did just that. Then there are the jobs advertised in in-house magazines and journals. These publications are not easy to get hold of unless you know someone who has access to them, but the major daily and Sunday newspapers have media pages, and specific trade journals like *Broadcast* or *The Stage* run advertisements. Start there.

You also need to promote yourself. Contact local cable TV and agree to do anything in order to get the experience and a foot in the door. Once you are in, you are a step nearer the camera. Offer radio reports to a local station. If your aim is to be a newscaster, then send audio cassettes of your own news bulletins. Likewise sports reports, cookery features or more generalised magazine formats (keep the total recording short, 5–6 minutes maximum). Once your voice is well known in the area via radio, the local TV station might start to take an interest in you. Whatever you do, don't just apply for the major jobs. Yes, you may be the lucky one – a 'star is born' perhaps once in 10,000 applicants – but don't hold your breath. Go for everything you think you can do. But if the advertisement asks for a scientist and you don't know an atom from an articulated truck, don't apply! No one will thank you for wasting their time, and some producers have long memories.

Seize every opportunity to present or MC an event. It not only gives you experience and confidence but just as importantly 'ups' your profile. More people will get to see you and know of you.

You'll notice that more often than not, an advertisement for a TV presenter will say, 'Please send your showreel'. When you've done very little recording or none at all this seems unreasonable but it's what producers want. From watching the showreels they make a shortlist, and if they like what they see you will be asked to audition. So, you need a showreel.

PUTTING TOGETHER YOUR SHOWREEL

The importance of your showreel cannot be underestimated. It is more than just a calling card, it is your first audition.

Your showreel should:

- give a good impression of what you look like on screen. The first 15 seconds are crucial
- show your personality
- demonstrate your professional abilities. For instance – interviewing skills, talking to camera, reading the news, demonstrating
- illustrate a couple of special skills or a specialised knowledge. For instance – sky diving, gardening, car maintenance, music, astronomy.

Think very carefully about what you want to show of yourself. Don't be rushed or rail-roaded by a production company simply because they have a format that they always use, or time is limited. The production standard of your showreel will depend on how much money you are willing to spend and invest in yourself. As there are hundreds of hopefuls sending in their tapes for the one advertised job, yours must stand out. A polished product will show the level of your commitment to your chosen vocation. My advice is not to skimp on your personal promotion; if you are successful then your first job will pay for any initial outlay. So if you have the funds, go to a professional studio with your own scripts and presentation ideas. However, if your finances are truly limited then there are alternatives.

(1) If you don't have any professionally recorded material then you will have to record something specially for the showreel. Use the best home video camera you can find, since anything less will produce a poor picture and will be difficult to edit. Depending on your style you can make a very effective showreel using a hand-held roving camera, but remember that it's you the producer wants to see, not flashy camera work. Include a piece speaking directly to a locked off (stationary) camera. Check your location and surroundings very carefully so that your set doesn't look too amateur. For instance, watch out for flowers which seem to come out of your head or indiscreet photographs on the shelf behind you. Look out for busy wallpaper patterns or clashing colours, and be equally aware of bright white backgrounds which can flare and look so glaring that they dominate the image. If you're filming outside, keep an eye on what is going on behind you and get someone to listen out for strange or intrusive noises. Review your presentation with a critical eye before you send it out and re-record if necessary. This is your first and perhaps your only opportunity to make an impression.

(2) Hire a professional quality camera and record yourself presenting a variety of items, with one or two outside shots. Find a camera operator who knows what they're doing. Do make sure that the lighting is good and that the pieces you present are edited together seamlessly. If you can't get rid of the crude end-of-programme jump, then make a feature of it.

(3) Presentation training courses often include a showreel in their price. As these are filmed in well-equipped studios they can look very professional and are likely to include magazine-style items, a news bulletin, a demonstration of some kind and an interview. However, there is a drawback. Quite often the courses run the same module in the same set, which means everyone ends up with their own version of the same programme. No intrinsic problem in that, except that a TV producer once confided in me that when he advertised for a presenter, one-third of the applicants had the same set, and some presenters appeared in three or four of the tapes as interview subjects. He said he began to get a fit of the giggles and found it hard to take any of them seriously. He suggested that if this is your only means of getting a showreel, then presenters should try to personalise or slightly alter the set by adding a few props or drapes and, if the course tutor allows, take along their own 'guest'.

(4) Some professional video production facilities offer to make up tapes for budding presenters. They advertise in most media journals; you can also find them in telephone directories and on the Internet. They will film set-up shots and specially written scripts as well as edit – in pieces you have already recorded. Generally, they give plenty of advice and suggest a variety of effects and captions which give a professional finish. Often you can design your own set, choose the location, create a programme or simply edit together a few well-chosen pieces. Go with plenty of ideas, varied programme formats and changes in scenes and clothing, but be prepared to be flexible. These companies are generally experienced in knowing what works and what doesn't. They can also be quite expensive, so make sure that you've seen examples of work they've already recorded and that you're happy with their standard and style.

If you have professionally recorded broadcast extracts, choose the best clips and line them up 10 seconds before the start. Time is money and you don't want to waste precious minutes in the editing suite looking for that 'really good bit'. Decide on your running order before you get to the editing suite – again, this saves time. You may change your mind when you start to put the takes together. That's fine, but the better prepared you are beforehand, the more willing the engineer will be to help you. Plan carefully what you want to present and be your own producer.

Content

- The duration of your showreel should be about 4–6 minutes.
- Put an impressive or special item at the beginning of the tape. If a producer isn't hooked in the first 30 seconds they are unlikely to watch the whole showreel.
- Make sure your face is in just about every frame, and not the dog or your aunt. She may end up with the job! Don't include single shots of the person you are interviewing or waste valuable time on picturesque scenes.
- If you have any recorded material from professional broadcasting, use it. Get the Beta or digital copy: VHS dubbed off the TV at home can give a poor reproduction, and has to be re-recorded on to either Beta SP or digital for editing. Each re-recording reduces the quality, so start off with the best format.
- Use the best quality VHS tapes you can afford for dubbing on to.
- If your material includes work that you have done for a reputable TV company, then use their logo. It will give you credibility.

Some ideas for your showreel

Here are some suggestions to put on your showreel, if you don't have professional recorded material – or items to add to what you already have.

- A piece straight to camera, talking about yourself
- News, weather or travel items
- A sales pitch
- An advert
- A demonstration
- An interview
- Vox Pop
- You as a game-show host
- You as main presenter of a magazine-style programme, cutting to you as reporter, advertiser, demonstrator, etc.

If there is only one subject you are interested in presenting, or only one in which you are a specialist – such as cookery, animals, sports, health or children's programmes – then be specific in your choice of items for your showreel. That doesn't necessarily mean it has to be limiting. Each item you record, showing differing programme formats, could be themed to your particular specialist interest.

And don't rule out a moment of madness. In contrast to the straight presentation, you could show the relaxed, more natural you. You could show yourself bursting into natural laughter at making a mistake or you could show that you don't mind looking a twerp and that you're game for a laugh. For instance, make a crazy appearance in costume as a banana or a huge mobile phone. If you do take up this idea, and your dominant style is a serious one, put this in as a final item!

PACKAGING YOUR SHOWREEL AND RÉSUMÉ

Presentation is all. A battered cardboard cover with your name stuck over the trade name gives a very poor impression, even though the showreel itself may be eligible for a BAFTA award. Use a good, solid cover with your photograph on it. Alternatively, have a smart, eye-catching design. Whatever you choose make sure that your name and contact number are *clearly* visible and legible.

Add to your package a well-presented CV (curriculum vitae). This should summarise your education (school, college, university) and any relevant courses and qualifications. Add to it any experience of presenting. This doesn't have to be professional and it doesn't have to be in television, although of course that will help. If you are just starting out it's worth mentioning any radio presenting you have done, hosting of live events and any public-speaking experience. Also list your special skills and your favoured interests. Your CV should include your name and contact details, height and colouring. You may also wish to scan your photograph on to it, as well as on to your showreel cover. Do make sure your face is visible somewhere – the most common frame is head and shoulders (CU) but a shot from the waist up (MS) is quite acceptable. Remember, though, that your face should be the most important feature. Choose whichever picture flatters you the most, and is the most natural. Use a colour photograph: $10'' \times 8''$ is the preferred size.

Send everything *first class*, in a well-padded envelope. Having gone to all this trouble you want your showreel to land safely. Keep a record of what you've sent and to whom, as well as any response. When networking, do the same by keeping all the relevant business cards. Write down on the back something that will help you to remember the contact much later on, e.g. friend of Gail's; produced *The Lamp*; married to Sonja.

Don't expect to get your tape back. You're lucky if you do, but it's more realistic to write it off as a loss – or a gain. One day some other producer may 'happen' to pick up your tape from off the shelf and BINGO! The dream job is yours!

In summary

- Have a very clear idea of the image you want to project on your showreel.
- Plan carefully what you want to include.
- Have a running order.
- Check your location.
- Present the whole package professionally.

THE FIRST APPROACH

Sending in your showreel

Now that you have your showreel, you need to send it to someone. Initially, your approach will be to the producers of programmes you want to work for, or to the station heads of programming. Identify the production companies and call the main number for their addresses. Telephone numbers can be found by calling directory enquiries or searching the Internet. Keep a record of contact names in advertisements.

In your search for a job there will be a certain amount of cold calling. It's never an easy task and you have to be prepared for a less than friendly reception. When you do find the right person to talk to, they are not always responsive: keep on trying until someone is. It may happen that you call on the day that they are actually looking for someone just like you. Always be friendly and aware of people's available time. Find a balance between enthusiastic persistence and being a persistent nuisance.

Advertising yourself

It is essential that you do your own networking and actively promote yourself. Personal contact is vital. The old saying 'It's not what you know, it's who you know' couldn't be more apt. Nevertheless, simply relying on being seen in the right place at the right time is too haphazard and therefore you need to take further action. If you are starting to think of yourself as a professional – and more importantly, as a career presenter as opposed to a presenter for hire – then you need 'shop windows' in which to promote yourself.

Spotlight
This directory of presenters includes all ages, sexes, styles and experience. It's generally used as a reference book by producers from both broadcast TV companies and corporate video-makers. It costs about £100 to put in details of yourself and a photograph. To keep the costs down, the publishers currently reproduce only black-and-white photographs, but the quality is excellent and this is a very useful advertising space.

Websites and talking CVs
It's been said that a business without a website is like a house without a door. An extremely effective advertising tool, a website can be bought very cheaply and can display much more than just your photograph and resume. A neat web page could include a variety of still images of you presenting in different locations. You may wish to install sections of your showreel, and navigators to your voice-over credits and demo – or to any other associated sites you think might be of interest. A simple 45-second piece to camera introducing yourself can also be very effective.

The possibilities for a creative website are endless, so don't be afraid to be unique and daring. Having said that, whatever you choose to do, keep in mind that the information must be easily accessible both visually and technically. Use templates for structure and design. And most importantly, keep to your own presenting style and identity. As you market yourself, remember the kind of work you are hoping to get from this advert: it would be a waste of space to clutter the page with confusing messages about who you are.

Like any advertisement, it's crucial to keep your website well maintained. Ensure that the details of all your contacts and current commitments are up to date.

DO I NEED A PRESENTER'S AGENT?

It's not absolutely necessary to have an agent to begin with. When you've had some on-screen experience you may find it useful to have someone to promote you or to take care of enquiries both from the press and from prospective employers. Agents also hear about jobs that aren't generally advertised. Many are listed in *Contacts*, a *Spotlight* publication, and range from big international companies representing actors, directors, writers and celebrities as well as TV presenters, to personal managers who look after only a handful of people. Some presenters choose to employ a personal manager to look after only them. There are also agencies that represent TV presenters working in a specific field such as sports, and booking agents that represent presenters from a wide base – including top corporate executives who work the after-dinner speaker circuit. You need to find the right management for your career and not take the first offer you get.

Establish a personal rapport with any potential agent and find out if they are right for you. How well do they know your work? Who else do they represent? How successful are they? What makes them more suitable than any other? This is your career, so choose wisely. Some agents will ask you to sign a contract. Check it very carefully and if there's anything you don't like, question it. Agents can ask for commission on work of between 15% and 30% plus VAT. Not only is this your career, but it is also a business – if you are good at what you do and lucky enough to be successful, people will want to make money out of you. Any contract has to be mutually beneficial. It would be unwise to sign anything with which you are not 100% happy.

USEFUL PUBLICATIONS

Available in most High Street newsagents:
- *The Guardian* (Media pages)
- *The Times* (Media pages)
- *Broadcast*
- *The Stage*

Available from given addresses:
- *Spotlight on Presenters* – 7 Leicester Place, London WC2H 7BF
- *Contacts* – published by *Spotlight*, address as above (lists agents, TV studios and many contacts)
- *The White Book* (lists production companies, TV studios and many contacts) (Birdhurst Ltd)
- *PCR* (*Professional Casting Report*) – PO BOX 100, Broadstairs, Kent CT10 1UJ

SOME USEFUL ADDRESSES

- British Equity – Job Information Service, Guild House, Upper St Martin's Lane, London WC2 9EG
- BBC – Wood Lane, Shepherds Bush, London W12

- National Film and TV School – Beaconsfield Studios, Station Road, Buckinghamshire HP9 1LG
- Brighton Film School – 13 Tudor Close, Dean Court, Rottingdean, East Sussex BN2 7DF
- Zorian International – www.zorianinternational.com
- UCAS – www.ucas.com (university courses)
- Local Further Education Colleges and Evening Classes

25

The Screen Test
and Audition

With very few exceptions, you will be asked to audition for every new job. The terms 'audition' and 'screen test' are often interchangeable, but while both require you to perform or demonstrate your abilities, auditions do not necessarily involve filming the process. At a screen test, you will always be filmed. Auditions vary according to the nature of the programme, but all will involve a screen test at some point, as producers want to see how you relate to the camera and how well you respond to direction. You will be set several tasks; some you will be asked to prepare prior to the audition, and some will be given to you without any forewarning. It's part of the assessment to evaluate how quickly and inventively you can think on your feet. There are some small, yet invaluable, preparations you can undertake in order to second-guess what lies in store, and it's worthwhile spending some time on them. Here are a few personal preparation tips for before you enter the studio.

- Find out as much as you can about the style and content of the programme.
- Rehearse any item you are asked to prepare.
- Rehearse any segment you think you may be asked to present.
- Choose clothing appropriate to your style and to the programme.
- Allow plenty of time to travel to the studio. Try to be 5 or 10 minutes early, but certainly don't be late. Some people check out the location of the venue a couple of days in advance so that they know just how long the journey takes and where exactly the studio is.
- Refresh yourself. Go to the toilet, brush or comb your hair, redo your make-up and have a glass of water. (You might consider taking an energy drink with you or a small snack. Some auditions can go on for several hours before you can take a break.)
- Relax. Perform some stretching and breathing exercises. Practise a few vocal routines and do any self-reaffirming mantras you think will help you to focus.
- Remind yourself of the contact names.

- Remember that first impressions last.
- Go to reception, introduce yourself and wait to be called.
- Turn off your mobile phone!

The audition starts *now*. It's a big mistake to think it only begins when the camera is on you: once you enter the grounds of the studio you are on show, and how you relate to everyone around you may be noted. When you are nervous it's easy to become impatient or quick-tempered, taking out any minor inconveniences on the car park attendant or receptionist. It's not worth it – be patient. You will need all your energy for the audition and you never know who else is watching. There is generally a lot of waiting about, so use your time well. If you are given a script to prepare when you arrive, work on it immediately. Focus on your task.

Other auditionees will sometimes be present, and you may have to work through a series of tasks and co-present with them. Be generous and work together. Whilst you are waiting, be careful of what you say to each other. Be friendly and use the opportunity to glean information about the audition and other auditions coming up, but remember that this is not a social gathering – conserve your energy. It can be tempting to share complaints about your journey, the coffee, the lack of time to prepare, the floor manager's instructions and so on, but grin and bear all irritations. You can whinge all you like when you get home.

Not everything you will be asked to do will be filmed or in front of the camera, but it's wise to work as if it were. You may simply be interviewed or alternatively asked to play games with a bunch of 7 year olds: go with the flow and be prepared to do anything. Some presenters' nerves make them over-effusive and their eagerness and enthusiasm run away with them – resist this tendency. Calm down, don't act. Be natural at all times and, as soon as you can, start to enjoy yourself. BBC Talent offers the following advice:

'This is a chance for you to tell us about yourself and let your personality shine. Don't overact or shout at the camera; the TV is a very intimate object. It's possible to be fresh, vibrant and exciting without being 'over big' to camera. Interpret the information you are given. Think about what you are trying to say. Presenting is not reading to or talking at, but it is getting the message across in a charismatic and engaging way.'

The audition

Nine times out of 10 you will be asked to talk about yourself to camera for about a minute. It's a golden opportunity to shine, be yourself and relax, and it's something you can prepare and rehearse at home. Have the first line ready in your head as you are given your cue to start. Start straightaway and say your name clearly. You might like to begin with where you are from and then go on to mention your interests and hobbies. Choose aspects of yourself which are interesting and will catch attention. Be selective and don't ramble on with a long list of credits and qualifications. Producers don't need to hear how wonderful their programme is, either – find one aspect of it that you identify with and build on that. Frequently you will be asked to ad lib or read from the autocue. Here are a few example auditions.

Example 1 – children's presenter
(1)   Introduce yourself to camera in 30 seconds.
(2)   Do a 45-second link, expanding the following information. You will be counted in and out of the piece:

● at 3.00 – *Pondlife*. A new series of the children's drama
● at 3.30 – *Buttercup Park*. Cartoon fun, main characters Daisy, Tulip, Wallflower and Turtle
● at 3.40 – *Catch*. Activity games show

Coming up now, it's the latest video from *Schools Out* . . .
(3)   Whilst playing tag with the rest of the group, explain how to play snakes and ladders.
(4)   Prepare a 2-minute piece to camera about school lunchtime.

Example 2
(1)   Filmed outside and walking towards camera, talk about why exercise is good for you. This should last 40 seconds.
(2)   Prepare a piece to camera on your favourite sports person, movie star or musician. This should last 30 to 40 seconds. You will be counted in and out of the item.
(3)   Using an earpiece, interview a fellow auditionee. You may choose any topic. The interview will last about 2 minutes. (Throughout this exercise you will be asked to cut short or lengthen the interview. You may also receive instructions on what to say and do via the earpiece.)

The screen test – what they say

'If you ever get the chance to do a screen test, the essential thing is to be natural. I was asked to imagine being outside a supermarket in South America. I read something about the area I was in and then put that into my own words. Then I just did it to camera, walking and talking looking into the camera. It was very traumatic, having never done anything like that before.'
Trevor Nelson (MTV, BBC Radio 1)

'We were given lots of tasks which didn't have anything to do with the programme. They just wanted to see how adaptable you were. We were doing a piece to camera and they were throwing oranges at us. Our brief was to react to the orange, not lose the viewer, and carry on talking. Just feel really confident that you can do it and you've got what it is they want.'
Kevin Duala (BBC Holiday, Nickelodeon)

'It was an absolute disaster. I still can't even begin to describe it, it's just too much of a painful memory: suffice it to say I felt like I had wasted everyone's time. But Chris Bellinger, who was then *Live and Kicking*'s editor, had other ideas.'
Jamie Theakston talking to BBC Talent (Live and Kicking, The Priory, Top of the Pops)

'You've just got to be able to take direction and respond to cues. Someone will come into a sterile booth and just *have it*. Others have nothing at all.'
BBC Producer Melanie Brown-Jones (at BBC Talent)

'You've got 3 minutes – you've got to give immediately. There are so many bland presenters, it's hard to find someone who is just different.'
BBC Producer Carolyn Clancey (at BBC Talent)

26

'How I Started' and Hot Tips from the Presenters

Matthew Kelly

'TV presenting wasn't something I set out to do. I started as an actor working in theatre and then TV. Whilst I was doing a sit com called *Holding the Fort* I was asked to host the TV quiz *Punch Lines*. They wanted a celebrity, and although I didn't feel like I was one, I wanted to keep working. Within three months everyone knew my first name. I had a straight choice: to be an actor or a TV personality. I was told no one would take me seriously as an actor again. I still do theatre though. Being successful isn't always useful. You have to top the last job you did or at least be equal to it. And then you are always wondering what happens next.'

Hot tip

'My advice is to really persevere. Do amateur stuff until it comes out of your ears. Practise to gain confidence, and experiment – find out what works for you. Keep educating yourself. It doesn't matter what, I did an Open University degree in contrasting religions. Do your homework and make sure you know what you're talking about, but never assume you know what the audience is thinking. I think you should have integrity. Above all be honest.'

Debbie Greenwood

'My father was a policeman, my mother a doctor's receptionist. We lived on Merseyside where my life couldn't have been further removed from TV presenting. I got into it purely by accident. I was Miss Great Britain and I was interviewed on BBC *Breakfast Time*. They thought I was articulate and liked me. I was interested in current affairs and so they offered me a spot to review the papers. I was then offered a job at Granada: they were very kind to me, and it was closer to home with more money. I was very naive and just took what was offered. I did a series called *Debbie Investigates*. I was terrified, but you get over it!'

Hot tip
'It's really important to develop a thick skin. It's a hard world and you have to toughen up. There's not always a clear reason why one person gets a job and one doesn't – you may well have equal ability. Although you are offering yourself up to be rejected, it's best not to take it personally. Maintain your optimism. Don't underestimate the value of contacts – you can get a job purely on the grounds that you were the last person on the phone. Find any speciality and make yourself stand out in the crowd. In my case, for instance, the producers thought it was unusual to find a beauty queen with a degree. Radio seems a very good background to train in: you learn to control a programme and how to interview, and you master the skill of talking to time.'

Julie Peasgood
'I was on *Pebble Mill* being interviewed as an actress and they gave me this revolting doll to talk about. After the programme I was summoned to the producer. I thought I was in for a reprimand but I was asked to present a TV review which I did for a year and that launched me into TV presenting.'

Hot tip
'Research your interview. I think it's important to memorise people's names. On a shoot, get to know as many names as possible, it's just courtesy. In fact, good manners are important all the time.'

Cheryl Baker
'I came in through the back door. At the height of my career with Bucks Fizz I was often invited on to chat shows; I seemed to be the most chatty of the group. I was asked to present *How Dare You* for Tyne Tees TV.'

Hot tip
'Be yourself, know your strengths and weaknesses and work to improve both.'

Jeremy Vine

'Initially I just wanted to be a reporter. I took an English degree and as a student I worked for hospital radio, local radio, student newspapers. After a spell at Coventry Evening News I joined the BBC. During a two-year traineeship I worked for TV and radio news programmes. From there I went on to work as a researcher on *Heart of the Matter*, as a reporter of R4's *Today* programme, and then as a presenter on *PM, Breakfast News, News Talk* and *Newsnight*.'

Hot tip
'Try to keep anchored to the real world, it's very easy to lose touch. The best presenters are natural presenters – someone who has something interesting about them, has been around the world and seen a fair bit, and who is aggressive when they need to be. Be extremely curious, too: read poetry, learn German, educate yourself. Being on the side of the viewer is also most important.'

Kirsten O'Brien

'Whilst I was a student I did hospital radio and local radio. I was experimenting, trying everything. I wanted to be the next Philip Schofield – I was very focused! I got a job as a PA on live news at Tyne Tees with a bit of researching. Then I presented a youth series programme, *What's On*, and put together a showreel which I sent to CBBC.'

Hot tip
'Just be yourself. Don't try to reinvent yourself. Gain as many skills as you can: PA, directing, researching, teamwork. Improve your concentration.'

Siân Lloyd

'After university, studying English and Celtic studies, I worked in commercial radio and then as a news researcher for *Wales Today*. Later, I presented a programme on harsh weather conditions and then, as I had news journalistic background, I was asked to present the weather bulletins. I wanted to know more so I took the Met (meteorology) exams, which for someone from the arts wasn't easy. I'm very proud of my qualification.'

Hot tip
'Get as much training as possible: I thoroughly enjoyed all the training I did. People want instant success, but you've got to be prepared to do anything. Concentrate and tell the story, chat to the viewer. It's surprising how people think they know you and make judgements about you, and it can be hard not to care whether they like you or not. You just have to get used to it and realise that you can't be liked by every-body.'

Jon Snow
'I didn't train. I saw an advertisement in *New Statesman* at LBC and did late-night phone-ins. I was the only one there without an accent so I got the job as a newsreader. I then got a job at ITN and whilst doing ITN bulletins I was asked to stand in for Peter Sissons at a moment's notice. Three months later I was still doing it and they gave me the job. It has all been fate. I was the right man in the right place at the right time.'

Hot tip
'Be open and honest. Don't act it, the viewer will see straight through you. You must be credible so that the news is seen as credible. Go off and cut your teeth as a reporter. Do as much TV journalism as possible and get experience. It's no good talking about things you have no knowl-edge of, the audience won't believe you.'

Kirsty Lang
'I studied politics at university and, wanting to be a reporter, became a graduate news trainee at the BBC. I learnt camera technique in the field but it's very different in a studio. I wanted to come in off the road and, whilst writing for the *Sunday Times* in Paris, a contact put me in touch with *Channel 4 News*.'

Hot tip
'Get jobs designed to lead you towards your goal. Be single-minded and show a real desire to ask questions. Take every opportunity and be tena-cious. Nurture your contacts – even just a phone call or brief e-mail to show that you are interested in them and their work.'

Matt Cain

'I got into doing drama at university whilst studying French and Spanish. I did the Edinburgh Festival and all that but I didn't have enough passion for theatre to have no money. Then I did a bit of production work for Granada Satellite before becoming a researcher for *BBC Choice*. We went to Majorca and no one on the crew spoke Spanish except for me, so I unwittingly ended up on camera, translating during a live show. Although I never thought I'd like it, I really enjoyed it. At *The Lab* and filming *020* I do a bit of everything in terms of directing, camera work, production, editing and presenting. Sometimes it's just me and the camera operator.'

Hot tip

'It's very risky if you only present. If you have other skills you can pitch ideas and have a really good idea of what works. Relax, enjoy and have lots of energy. I think a lot of it is having confidence.'

Sophie Raworth

'After completing degrees in French and German I took a postgraduate course in broadcasting and journalism and then joined the BBC's regional trainee scheme. I loved radio reporting and hated the idea of getting up on stage. When I did decide TV was for me it was as a producer. Being a TV presenter was a fluke really, I just happened to be at the right meeting when they were looking for a presenter/reporter for *Look North* in Yorkshire. Two years later I was presenting *BBC Breakfast News*.'

Hot tip

'If you want to be in news, you must be in journalism. Work in radio or TV news. Prove yourself as a reporter. Keep across as many subjects as you can all the time, making sure you are informed on virtually everything because you don't know from one day to the next what you will be doing.'

Simon McCoy

'I always wanted to be a journalist. I went to a journalist's college and trained as a print journalist, but always with a view to going into TV – it's where journalism seemed to me to be the best. Picture and sound is what it's all about. I worked for a news agency in Fleet Street and kept up my contacts with Thames TV where I got a job as a researcher and script editor. Then I was a news editor for *TV AM*. All the time I never appeared on screen and, getting quite frustrated, I came to *SKY* as a producer. I saw my chance when I became royal correspondent and presented news shifts. Now I present the news. It's fun – I've been through all the different disciplines.'

Hot tip
'If like me you know what you want, you just have to go for it. Knock on the door repeatedly until they get fed up of you. Once you get a foot in the door, which is the major hurdle, you make your own way. Get people's names right and spell them correctly. I know people who won't even open the envelope if they see their name mis-spelt. If you go into the business where accuracy is important you have to start on the right track.'

Huw Edwards

'As a postgraduate student, with every intention of being an academic, I worked on the student newspaper and local radio, principally reviewing opera. I started to enjoy my hobby rather than my given field of mediaeval French poetry. I saw an advert for the BBC news trainee course and applied on the off-chance. It's an eternal mystery to me how I got it. My two big interests were politics and music and the one thing I wanted to do was work for *BBC from Westminster*. I spent 10 years reporting from there as a political correspondent for both TV and radio. Then I presented the *One O'Clock, Six O'Clock* and *Breakfast News* programmes.'

Hot tip
'Have a network of people you can trust. I am convinced that an audience warms to a presenter who shows some warmth, humour and emotion when things are not so good, and who tries to bring them in using fairly direct language.'

Kate MacIntyre

'I always loved theatre, and knew I wanted to get into TV whilst I was at university, where I was doing geography. I had a real passion for it. I took a year off after university and travelled the world. From different places I would send postcards to TV producers back in the UK saying where I was. I'd never met them before, they were working on programmes I was interested in. When I got back, I got some interviews and became a runner for *Wish You Were*

Here. I'd do anything. I begged them to let me have a go at reporting and got my big break in Paris. Having told everyone I could do it with my eyes shut, I then had to prove myself, it was very scary.'

Hot tip
'Persevere. It's a nightmare trying to get jobs, and it's good to have lots of friends. I came down from Warrington with no money and there wasn't much left over from my wages – London is very expensive. My friends gave me a floor to sleep on and really helped me to get by. Be very focused and keep going until you get your break.'

Trevor Nelson

'I was just a fan of music, mad about it from about 12 or 13. I worked on Kiss FM when it was a pirate station and then it went legal. Then I went to Radio 1. A producer who worked at Radio 1 was then working as head of programming at MTV and she'd heard my show, thought that I'd be good for MTV.'

Hot tip
'Never ever base yourself on someone else. Be an individual. It's the perfect time to learn your trade with digital TV and then break through; there's nothing worse than baptism on a terrestrial channel, since you're on and off like, yesterday, and no one will ever hear of you again. If you do want to be the consummate professional, you have to be versatile. Always remember your audience – I'm always aware of who's listening and who's watching. It's a key thing. Research properly, and never lose your personality.'

Paul Coia

'I started at university, with student TV. Then I tried my hand at all the different, related jobs – I approached local TV and radio and began doing continuity announcing for STV. The desk was just a plank of wood balanced on my knees with a clock by the side of the TV monitor. From there, I got the job as senior announcer at Channel 4.'

Hot tip
'Learn everything. Learn what everyone does. Learn what happens so that if there's a break in the chain you know what's going on. Never forget that it's a team effort.'

Kevin Duala

'I trained as a dancer and was in *Starlight Express* but didn't see my career going on as a dancer. I had no idea how to get into presenting. I sent out my video to loads of agents. One got back to me saying they were full but inviting me in for a chat. I went away determined to get a job and go back. Eventually I gatecrashed an audition for a live children's programme. There were hundreds of people, whittled down to four of us – and I got the job.'

Hot tip

'I think you've got to have hunger and know that it's what you want to do. If you go into it thinking, well, I'm not really too sure, you're never going to be desperate enough. You've just got to make them keep watching. You've got to be able to think on your feet.'

Lisa Aziz

'Everything came together when I was at university. I was news editor of the student newspaper and was asked on to LBC to talk about a piece I'd written on the Deptford fire. I realised I loved the whole broadcast element. I had this urge to ask the questions. I wrote hundreds and hundreds of handwritten letters. One person replied from Liverpool Radio City and said, 'Come in and see me if you're passing.' I pretended I was passing. I had 20 minutes to sell myself and at the end of 20 minutes he said I'd got the traineeship. It was all go, tough stories, hard work. After a year I wrote to TV companies, I wanted to be a TV reporter. I treated letter-writing as a job; I'd call the boss of the company. I got a job at BBC Bristol, then was poached by HTV . . . and then TV-AM. I was on a roll!'

Hot tip

'Prove that you are a hard worker, and committed. Have a very clear idea about your strengths and what you want to do. I don't hold that just because you are popular you can do everything – you have to know in your heart that you are comfortable with it. You'll get easily bored if the job isn't what you are interested in.'

Suzi Perry

World Super Bike was a sport I just loved. I loved watching it. I thought, 'they didn't really listen to what he said,' and 'he should have asked this or that.' I was a bit Bolshie really. I went to SKY and said I could do this. They had a look at me and said."OK. Start at Brands Hatch." I was the first female reporter in the sport, in the world.

Hot tip

Be determined and able to take criticism. If you want longevity then you have to know what you're talking about. You want to be a bit different and a bit dedicated. When interviewing there's no point planning things with kids or old people.

Jeff Moody

'I got a degree in English and Drama. I really wanted to be an actor, but by about the third day I realised I wasn't very good. In fact, I couldn't act my way out of a paper bag. Searching for a job in the *Guardian*, I went for a job as an autocue operator at ITN. I looked at it as a foot in the door. After about 6 months I got a screen test for a job as children's presenter. I was in America but I came back because they said they liked the look of me. I took a gamble and came back and got the job – as a children's presenter with a glove puppet called 'Smelly'. That ended, and I was at a very low point. I worked on Selena Scott's show for two years as a producer, researcher and writer and found that invaluable. Following a long period of unemployment I had to go back to square one and work as an autocue operator; I had a real sense of failure. Then, at very short notice, I screen tested to do the weather, covering for the regular man.'

Hot tip

'You may make it tomorrow or in a year's time, in 20 years' time or maybe longer. You may be like me, wallpapering your room with rejection letters, stuffing envelopes with showreels and sending them out only to get letters back from people who haven't even had the courtesy to look at your tape. And that will keep on happening time and time again. But if you just keep going you will get there. You just have to have constant belief in yourself. Get work experience (which means working for nothing), know all the other roles and get experience in the area you want to work in. When a position comes up, you will know what to do.'

Glossary – Insider's Jargon

I have discovered that technicians and production teams love abbreviations and pet names, so here's a translation of some you may come across. You'll find them not only in conversation but littered across your script. There are many others, so please feel free to add your own discoveries.

Action Cue for the presenter or action to start given by director when camera and sound are running up to speed.

Ad Lib Unscripted, improvised speech.

AFM Assistant floor manager.

ANNCR The station announcer or continuity person.

ANNO Announcer or announcement.

Archive material Footage from library or file.

Aston Brand name for a TV caption generator. Operated from the gallery or editing suite.

Aston Super Titles and captions can be superimposed on the picture.

Autocue Brand name for a speaker prompt, the system that enables you to read the script spooled up in front of the camera lens.

A/V Alternate viewing (i.e. what's on the other channels).

A/V Audio visual.

Back Anno A spoken reference to the last item(s) just broadcast.

Backing track A pre-recorded audio track, music or sound effects over which it's possible to sing or speak.

Barn doors Black metal flaps fixed to lights to assist light direction.

Blocking Moves of presenter, guests and cameras worked out before recording.

Boom Long telescopic pole from which a microphone is suspended.

BOP Beginning of part.

Breakthrough Unwanted sound breaking through the audio channel.

Call Sheet (Shooting schedule) Details of times and location for everyone concerned.

CAM Camera.

Camera Script List of shots and details needed by camera crew.

Cans Headphones.

In the can Recording is complete.

Caption card (CAP) A card on which can be mounted pictures, words or any artwork, then placed on the caption stand for the camera to focus on. Useful for a steady picture.

CAP GEN Caption generated from ASTON.

CB Centre break, commercial break.

Crawler Caption or message that runs across the screen.

Chroma key (CSO, CK) An electronic device that selects a colour and, when shooting against that colour, can fill in with pictures from another source. Blue is usually the chosen colour, as it's most distant from flesh tones, but any colour can be used. The presenter should not wear the chroma-keyed colour as the picture from the alternative source will appear to show 'through' them. Most often used in weather reports.

Clip A short extract of film or video.

Clock (VT clock) A clock face which appears before the start of programme or video tape. It includes programme/item details as well as technical information. Operates as a countdown and fades to black 3 seconds before zero in case it is accidentally selected to go on air.

Colour bars Colour strips which TV engineers use to test the transmission.

COMM Voice-over commentary.

COMMS Commercial break.

Cue Dot (Q Dot) Electronic square at the corner of the screen, signalling commercial breaks or end of programme. Usually appears 30 seconds before the change and disappears 5 seconds before the change.

Cut A sharp finish to the filming.

Cut away A shot showing detail or reaction which is later cut into the programme during editing.

CYC (Cyclorama) Large backing cloth for the set, disguising studio wall.

Cue Action instruction – Stand by & cue; Cue & mix; Cue & cut. Presenter goes on the cue. The other instructions are for the director or vision mixer.

Mix (Dissolve) A sound or vision fade transition into another sound or picture.

DLS Digital library store.

Dolly A trolley for a camera, helping it to move smoothly.

Domestic cut-off The frame of the TV in most homes is smaller than that seen in the studio, so some parts of the picture will be 'cut off'.

Down the line An interview with participants in different locations, listening to each other on earpieces or speakers but not necessarily seeing each other.

Dub Transferring recorded sound and vision on to another tape.

DUR. Duration (RT – Running Time).

Dry run Rehearsal without cameras.

DVE Digital video effect.

Earpiece Piece of clear plastic moulded to fit the ear so that you can receive talkback and instructions from the gallery.

EB End break (end of programme).

E/C End credits.

ENG (Portable single camera – PSC) Electronic news gathering. Uses lightweight video camera.

EOP End of part (of programme).

EQ System to equalise and balance sound.

Establishing shot (GV) A general view of a location.

Eyeline The direction in which the presenter, guest or artist is looking.

Feedback (Howling, Howlround) A screaming sound caused by a microphone picking up its own amplified sound from speakers or headsets.

Fire lane A painted line on the studio floor, marking a passage which must not be blocked.

Fish-eye lens A very large wide-angled lens.

Flat A flat piece of scenery.

FM Floor manager.

Foldback Sound fed through to the studio.

Follow up A report based on a previously broadcast item.

Format Programme style.

Freeze frame One frame of the picture of film 'frozen', stilled on tape.

FX Effects (SFX – sound effects).

FVO Female-voice over.

Gaffer tape Wide sticky tape used for heavy duty jobs e.g. binding cables together or sticking them to the studio floor.

Gallery A soundproofed room from where all sound and vision is operated and controlled.

Generation First generation is the master video copy. Once it's been dubbed on to another tape it becomes second generation, third, fourth and so on, degenerating as the process is repeated.

Goldfishing Term used to describe someone on screen who is seen to be talking but not heard.

Grams. Off disc (originates from 'off the gramophone'!).

Green room (Hospitality suite) Where programme participants wait to be called to the studio.

Gun Mic/Rifle Mic Microphones.

GTS Greenwich Time Signal.

GV General View.

Handbasher Portable light often used for outside broadcasting (OB).

Headroom Amount of space above a person's head in camera frame.

Hold (Tease) A promo for the programme coming up after a commercial break or after the next programme. It's an advert intended to 'hold' the audience to that given channel.

Hook up Open conference line between national presentation departments or OBs.

Intro./Lead in Introduction. First sentence of an item.

IN VIS or I/V In vision.

Key light The main light focusing on person or set. You, the presenter need to know where this falls so that you will always be properly lit.

Jump cut A jarring edit which doesn't quite match up.

Junction Link point from one item to another.

LD Lighting designer or director.

Leader The run-in part of the audio, film or video tape which cannot be recorded on to but gives time for machines to run up to speed.

Library music (Mood music) Effects and music not for sale but used under licence.

Live Real time.

Locked off Camera movement fixed into a stationary position.

LS (LVS) Lighting supervisor (Lighting & Vision).

LS Camera long shot.

Master tape Finished programme, edited and ready for broadcast.

MCR Master Control Room (all transmission goes through here).

Mic Microphone.

Mix (Dissolve) A sound or vision fade transition into another sound or picture.

Mixer Technical piece of equipment operational for mixing or cutting pictures, or for audio mixing quality and level of sound.

Monitor TV screen which shows broadcast quality 'off air' programme, video or film. In the studio you can keep a check on what is going on. In presentation suites there's often several monitors showing what's coming on air (live transmission), what's on air, what other TV channels are showing.

MS Camera mid-shot.

MS Master shot. A wide, back-up shot of scene or studio set-up or action e.g. cooking, orchestra, band, sport, in case the cutaway doesn't work or MS is preferred.

Mute shot Vision without sound recorded.

MVO Male voice-over.

NIBS News in brief.

N/W Next week.

Noddy (Cut-away) A shot of a reporter or of the 'listener' nodding at the speaker or interviewee. It's used in editing to vary the picture or cover any shot that doesn't work. In location news filming 'noddies' are often used as there's usually only one camera.

OB Outside broadcasting.

OC On camera.

Off line A rough edit or poor quality replay used to check the look or duration of a piece of programme.

OOV Out of vision.

Opt out When a region decides to put in a programme of their choosing over nationally networked programmes – e.g. local news – the regional station will opt out of a national networked programme. They then OPT back IN to the national network.

Out takes Recorded but unused material.

Out cue Last words or picture to cue next item. Very important for cuts and for links. (SOC – Standard Out Cue – the regular final words. 'And that's it from me' or 'Joanne Zorian, *Holiday News*').

Outro (the out) Final words (5–15 seconds) of a programme.

PA Production Assistant.

P2C – Piece to camera A report or statement spoken straight to camera.

Popping Explosive sound when speaker is too close to the microphone.

POV Point of View shot. A shot taken from the viewpoint of whatever, whoever it is you're filming (e.g. a dog, a child, the narrator).

Pres. Presenter.

Promo. Promotional trailer for a programme or film.

PSC Portable Single Camera.

Q Cue point.

Q Dot (Cue dot) Electronic square at the corner of the screen signalling commercial breaks or end of programme. Usually appears 30 seconds before the change.

Repo. A command to camera to reposition to a different location on set or pre-agreed angle.

Reverses A shot of the interviewer asking the questions, in much the same way as a 'noddy' is used. Generally taken on location after the interviewee has gone.

Rostrum camera Camera fixed to take shots of photographic items, news clippings, objects, graphics etc.

Running time (RT) Duration of the programme or segment of programme.

Rushes (Dailies) Unedited film.

RT Running time.

RX Recording date and/or time. Receiving data or programme material time.

Scanner Van used for outside broadcasts (OB) transmissions.

Scene dock Area close to the studio where props and scenery are stored.

SFX Sound effects.

Shooting schedule A list of locations, times and outlines of shots, as well as all personnel required and their calls.

Shot list List of all shots.

S/I Superimpose.

SOC – Standard Out Cue The regular final words. 'And that's it from me . . .'

SOF Sound on film.

SOOV Sound out of vision.

Sound bite Speech or words cut for greater impact.

SOVT Sound on video.

Squawk box Intercom system.

SS Sound supervisor.

Sting Short piece of music.

Storyboard Sketched picture of each shot giving visual indication of what, in story terms, is to be achieved.

TBA To be arranged. Details and information to be filled in later.

Tag Used at the end of promo trails, e.g. 'Tomorrow at 8'. Different versions (tags) are edited on. 'Tonight at 8 . . . In half an hour . . . Next'.

Talkback Sound link from gallery to studio via earpieces or headphones. **Lazy talkback** – a direct line from the presenter's mic, fed to a separate talkback speaker in the gallery, so that a two-way conversation can happen during a commercial break or VT inserts. **Open talkback** – a facility that allows everyone with earpieces or headphones to hear what's going on in the gallery. **Switch talkback** – where presenters can hear only what the director wants them to hear, i.e. directions. The director will then switch on to the presenter's earpiece.

Tease (Hold) A promo for the programme coming up after a commercial break or after the next programme. It's an advert intended to 'hold' the audience to that given channel.

Time code The exact timing of the video tape encoded on the tape but never broadcast. Makes editing and finding shots easier. Hours, minutes, seconds, frames are shown.

TM or TC Technical manager or technical co-ordinator.

Tone A sound used to line up audio equipment.

TX Transmission date/time.

VHS Video cassette.

VM Vision mixer.

VPVT Video tape seen on screen.

VR Virtual reality.

VT Videotape.

VO Voice-over. Out of vision speech or commentary (MVO – male voice-over; FVO – female voice-over).

Vox Pop *VOX POPULI* – Latin for 'voice of the people'. Generally, street interviews looking for a one-line sound bite from the general public.

VS (VERS.) Version.

VT (VTR) Videotape (videotape machine/recorder).

VTC Videotape control (where recorded programmes and segments are played from).

Wild track Recorded background sound, to add effect.

CAMERA SHOT ABBREVIATIONS

CAM CAP Camera caption.

CU Close-up.

BCU Big close-up.

GV General view.

L/A CU Low angle close-up (camera would be looking up at the subject).

LS Long shot.

VLS Very long shot.

MCU Medium close-up shot.

Mix Slow change from one picture to another.

MS Mid-shot.

Pan Camera moves horizontally or vertically in a smooth movement.

POV Point of View.

WA Wide angle.

Wipe A transition shot wiping over one picture with another.

WS Wide shot.

Appendix 1

Presenter's Survival Kit

Every presenter needs a survival kit for studio or location filming. This contains the basic, yet essential, items you may need and don't want to be rushing back to your dressing room for, or pestering a member of the crew to 'do you a favour' and get. It's useful to have everything together and in a bag which you keep at your desk and don't take home or 'borrow' from. Buy a wash bag or one of those clear plastic zip-folder pouches. I prefer clear plastic, as I can easily see what I'm looking for. Of course, there may be someone on hand to sew that button back on, powder your shiny nose and offer you water – but if there isn't, like every good girl guide and boy scout, *be prepared*. You will not need everything I've listed here; just select the items which you do need or use regularly.

Earpiece for talkback
Hairbrush or comb
Powder and pad
Essential make-up
Mirror
Toothbrush and toothpaste
Battery razor
Tissues
Mini sewing kit
Safety pin
Small bottle of water
Throat sweet or boiled sweet or mint
Pen or pencil
Highlighter pen
Paper clip
Stopwatch
Cue cards
Refresher tissue or small chamois leather and small bottle of Eau de Cologne
Don't forget a hard copy of your script.

Appendix 2

Sample Running Order and Script – Magazine-Style Show

NO.	ITEM	SOURCE/AREA	DUR.	RX.	TX.
	A	B	C	D	E
1	PART 1 OPENING TITLES	VT - 1	30"		
2	PRESENTER INTRO - Jon	STUDIO AREA - A	5"	35"	
3	PROGRAMME TRAILER	VT - MUTE PRES 1 & 2 V/O	15"	50"	
4	H. PRES. LINK TO CREATURES VT	STUDIO AREA - A	25"	1'15"	
5	CREATURES VT	VT - 2	2'10"	3'25"	
6	CREATURES INTERVIEW	INTERVIEW AREA - B	5'	8'25"	
7	LINK TO VT FILM TEASE	STUDIO AREA - A	10"	8'35"	
8	FILM TEASE VT	VT - 1	15"	8'50"	
9	LINK TO COMMS	STUDIO AREA - A	5"	8'55"	
10	EOP 1 STING	VT - 2	5"	9'00"	
11	PART 2 BOP/STING	VT - 2	10"	10"	
12	LINK TO RECIPE OF THE DAY	STUDIO AREA - A	15"	25"	
13	RECIPE OF THE DAY	KITCHEN AREA - C	5'	5'25"	
14	LINK TO VT FILM RELEASE	STUDIO AREA - A	15"	5'40"	
15	FILM RELEASES	VT - 1	2'18"	7'58"	
16	FILM INTERVEIW	STUDIO AREA - A	2'	9'58"	
17	FILM CHOICE	VT - 2	22"	10'20"	
18	GOODBYES & CLOSING	STUDIO AREA - A	20"	10'40"	
19	CLOSING CREDITS	VT - 1 + ASTON	15"	10'55"	

Key: RX - expected accumulated running time
TX - actual accumulated running time

191

Example of magazine-style script - Part One Only

(*See* Chapter 11, *Running Order and Script Layout*, and Glossary – *Insider's Jargon* for abbreviations.)

MORNING SOFA

			SOUND
SHOT 1. VT – 1 DUR: 30″			
ITEM 1 OPENING TITLES	SOVT		

SHOT 2. CAM 2 A. WS STUDIO TRACK IN TO 2 SHOT

ITEM 2 PRES JON & HELENE			
(S/BY VT 2)	HELENE	Hello. Good morning and there's plenty to keep us afloat in today's programme.	
RUN VT			

SHOT 3. VT – 2

ITEM 3			
	JON	Yes it's a watery theme as Helene proves when she dons a wetsuit and takes the plunge.	MUTE & V.O.
	HELENE	Francis is cooking up a seafood special to tickle our taste buds.	
	JON	And Marsha Church has news of all the latest film releases and gives us – guess what? – yes, a review of the ocean bound adventure, TIDAL WAVE.	

SHOT 4 CAM 2 A. SHOT MCU PRESENTERS

ITEM 4 LINK TO VT CREATURES

	JON	So Helene, what exactly have you been up to?
(S/BY VT 1)	HELENE	Everyone has their own personal image of pure relaxation. Mine is swimming in warm, sunlit tropical waters. Or diving amongst angel fish and coral reeefs. Or it was, until I met up with Doctor Peter Ashley, an oceanic scientist and explorer of the Deep. This is what he told me about
RUN VT		CREATURES OF THE ABYSS.

SHOT 5. NT 1.

ITEM 5 CREATURES   SOVT

IN WORDS –

HELENE &
CAMERAS   '6 miles beneath the surface we have
MOVE TO   only just started to . . .
INTERVIEW
AREA)

Dur: 2′10″

OUT WORDS –
. . . and just when you thought you
were safe.'
OUT VIS. – Bubbles under the water.

SHOT 6. CAM.2 B. 2 SHOT PRES. & GUEST – INTERVIEW AREA

ITEM 6 CREATURES INTERVIEW

| | HELENE | It really is the stuff of wild adventure films. And most of us are unlikely to enounter those aquatic monsters. I say most, because I'm joined by |

SHOT 7. CAM 1 B. MCU PROF (Guest)

| | Professor Janet Eccles who is organising an expedition in search of these creatures. |

SHOT 8. CAM 2 B. 2 SHOT

	Hello Janet. Welcome to MORNING SOFA. What do you hope to
AS DIRECTED:	find?
CAM. 1. GUEST	
CAM.2. 2 SHOT	AD LIB INTERVIEW
CAM 3. HELENE	

TOWARDS END OF INTERVIEW RELEASE CAM
2 TO PRESENTER JON

SHOT 9 CAM 3 B. HELENE

| | Thank you for coming in to talk to us. |
| | Now back to you Jon. |

SHOT 10 CAM 2 A. MCU JON

ITEM 7 LINK FILM TEASE

JON	AD LIB BACK REF ON INTERVIEW.
(S/BY VT 1)	Coming up after the break we've Francis in the Kitchen and Marsha brings us all the latest film news including the gossip on this one.
RUN VT	

SHOT 11. VT 1

ITEM 8 FILM TEASE – TIDAL WAVE   SOVT

	IN WORDS: VISUAL – ROUGH SEAS.
	'Where's the Captain? . . .
	DUR: 00.15″

OUT WORDS: . . . Oh no, no!
Tell me it's not true!'
OUT VIS. – Woman looks up.

SHOT 12 CAM.2 A 2 SHOT PRES. JON & HELENE

ITEM 9 LINK TO COMMS

(S/BY VT2)　　　　　AD LIB:

　　　　　　　　HELENE　　Exciting!
RUN VT　　　　JON　　　　We'll see you after the break.

SHOT 13 VT 2 END OF PART 1 STING　　DUR: 5″

ITEM 10　　　　　　　　　　　　　　　　　　　　　　SOVT

<u>END OF PART 1</u>

Appendix 3

Exercises – News in Brief (NIBS)

EXERCISE 1

SOUND

SHOT no 1. OPENING CREDITS VT 1.   Dur: 10″
***

ITEM 1   SOVT

SHOT 2. CAM 1 A. MCU PRES. NEWSSTUDIO
***

ITEM 2

(ST/B VT 1)**Presenter** RUN VT	Good afternoon and welcome to the lunchtime news.

SHOT 3. VT – 2headlines.   PRES. VO

ITEM 3   Within the last hour it's been
announced that the entire workforce at
the Hutch and Kennels look set for
redundancy. The company now says its
order books are empty and survival
now depends on winning a contract to
build garden sheds.

SHOT 4. CAM 1.A MCU
***

(S/BY VT 1)   A spokesman said that they were
surprised by their recent losses but
were extremely hopeful of a bright
RUN VT   future.

SHOT 5.VT – 1 Observatory
***

ITEM 5   PRES. V/O

A dramatic rescue took place today on

196

the banks of the River Dee in Little Croft near Chester. Fire fighters, the police and the RSPCA were all involved in pulling out a pony and a cow which both got stuck in the mud beside the river. No one knows how the two animals got there but after 8 and half hours petrified, cold and caked in mud they were hauled to safety.

SHOT 6. CAM 1.AMCU PRES. STUDIO

ITEM 6

(SLIDE)

(S/BY VT 2)

RUN VT

The acclaimed British film WHERE BIRDS FLY, has been tipped for 4 Academy Awards nominations – best actor, best actress, best original screenplay and best original dramatic score as well as achievements in technical excellence.
And finally ....

SHOT 7. VT 2 PONY TAIL

ITEM 7

A serial snipper has been caught in Melbourne Australia after cutting off a woman's pony tail on a train. Police found a hoard of 11 ponytails hidden in his flat, thought to date back a decade or more. The 34 year old scissorhands said he had approached women in the street offering them £500 for their hair but when they wouldn't accept his offer, he found another means of adding to his collection.

SHOT 8. CAM 1. AMCU PRES. STUDIO

ITEM 8
(ST/B VT 1)

That's it for this edition on LUNCHTIME HEADLINES.

```
                              Next News is at 3.30.
          RUN VT             Good Afternoon.

VT 1 CLOSING CREDITS     DUR:6″                              SOVT

ITEM 9
```

EXERCISE 2

Find yourself a newspaper. Search out the NEWS IN BRIEF section or edit a longer article to create a story of 50–70 words. Choose three or four and practise reading a news bulletin.

EXERCISE 3

Once you've read the following chapters on reading the weather and travel news, start to combine different items. You can use the example scripts to practise with, but it's easy to create your own.

Practise handing over to an imagined co-presenter, or get a friend or relative to join in and share the news between you.

'Time to take a look at the transport and traffic picture, a travel update with Andy.'

'And now over to Gary with the latest sports news.'

'Coming up now with news from the City, Joan.'

'Will the sun shine on us today? To tell us which way the wind blows, over to Elizabeth.'

'And that's how the roads look this evening. Back to Ruth.'

'Exciting matches to watch this evening. I return you now to our own super athlete, Adam.'

'So the economic trend is on an up. Good news for all of us . . . Mary.'

'I'm off to the beach now to catch some of that very welcome, warm, sunny weather – leaving you with Eric. Goodbye for now.'

Further Reading

BODY LANGUAGE AND VISUAL PRESENTATION
The Naked Ape, Desmond Morris, Jonathon Cape
The Complete Style Guide from Color Me Beautiful Organisation, Mary
   Spillane, Piatkus
Style Guide for Men, Mary Spillane, Piatkus
Body language. How to read others thoughts by their gestures, Allan Pease,
   Thorsons

RELAXATION AND FIGHTING FEARS
Feel the Fear and Do it Anyway, Susan Jeffers, Fawcett Books
The Little Book of Calm, Penguin
101 Essential Tips - Relaxation, Nitya Lacroix & Deni Brown, Dorling
   Kindersley

VOICE TRAINING
Clear Speech, Malcolm Morrison, A & C Black
The Right to Speak, Patsy Rodenburg & Ian McKellen, Routledge
Your Voice and How to use it Successfully, Cecily Berry, Harrap Books

VOICE OVERS
Making Money in Voice Overs, Terri Apple & Gary Owens, Long Eagle
   Publishing
Voice Overs, Bernard Graham Shaw, A & C Black
TV and Radio Announcing, Stuart Hyde, Houghton Miffin

TV PRODUCTION
Understanding Television, Andrew Goodwin & Gary Whannel, Routledge
Television Production, Gerald Millerson, Focal Press

FACING THE MEDIA
Surviving the Media, Diana Mather, Thorsons
Total Exposure, Gustav Carlson, Amacom
A Career Handbook for TV, Radio, Film, Video & Interactive Media, Shiona
   Llewellyn, A & C Black

PRESENTERS AUTO BIOGRAPHIES
Is it Me? - Terry Wogan, BBC Worldwide Ltd
Oprah, an autobiography, Oprah Winfey

Index